Quiet Excellence

52 REFLECTIONS ON WORK, FAITH & WHAT TRULY MATTERS

Quiet Excellence

52 REFLECTIONS ON WORK, FAITH & WHAT TRULY MATTERS

Rajneesh Jain

Om EDGE
An Imprint of Om Books International

First published in 2026 by

Om>
EDGE An Imprint of Om Books International

Corporate & Editorial Office
A-12, Sector 64, Noida 201 301
Uttar Pradesh, India
Phone: +91 120 477 4100
Email: editorial@ombooks.com
Website: www.ombooksinternational.com

Sales Office
107, Ansari Road, Darya Ganj,
New Delhi 110 002, India
Phone: +91 11 4000 9000
Email: sales@ombooks.com
Website: www.ombooks.com

ISBN: 978-93-6395-531-8

Printed in India

10 9 8 7 6 5 4 3 2 1

Contents

Message: Sri Sri Ravi Shankar ix
Foreword: Mohanbir Sawhney xi
Introduction: Srinivasa Prasad xv
Praise for the Book: Ashishkumar Chauhan xvii
Praise for the Book: BK Asha xix
Preface xxi

Part 1: The Little Things That Change Everything

1. The Big Deal That Cost Just ₹10 3
2. The Puppy Who Taught Me About Anger Management 6
3. Keep Shining Anyway 10
4. The Keys to a Happy Life 14
5. The Mess We Make 18
6. A Pinch of Spice 22
7. Letting Go of Fear 25

Part 2: Work, Leadership & Quiet Grace

8. The Leader as Teacher 31
9. The 5% Club 35
10. BHEL: The First Chapter I Still Revisit 39
11. Live Like the Coconut Tree 43
12. Seedism: The Wisdom Hidden Underground 47
13. Unheard Today, Unforgettable Tomorrow 51

Part 3: Gratitude, Roots & the People Who Shape Us

14. The Unsung Ones Who Hold Us Up 57
15. The Ones Who Wait 60
16. The Three People We Carry Within 63
17. The Little Eyes Watching Us 67
18. The Shoulders We Stand On 71

Part 4: Inner Peace, Faith & Emotional Courage

19. Where Peace Begins: A Personal Note on Letting Go 77
20. Inner Intelligence (II): Seeing What We Already Have 81
21. GOD Chat 84
22. Stay True to Yourself 87
23. The Gift of a Well-Placed "No" 91

Part 5: India, Wisdom & the Collective Soul

24. Ten Lessons I Brought Back from the Mahakumbh 97
25. Where Are You Going So Fast? 101

26. How India Played Its Way to Health 105
27. Build a Business on Worth, Not a Gamble 108
28. Trust the Process 112

Part 6: Karma, Choices & Moral Clarity

29. Don't Forget Your Hanumans 117
30. Exercise or Excuse? You Choose 120
31. Where the Water Gets In 124
32. Less Is Enough 128
33. The Price Is Yours 133
34. The Circle Always Closes 138
35. The Poison of Assumptions 143
36. Ek Ruka Hua Faisla (A Pending Decision) 148

Part 7: Faith, Growth & the Long View

37. Many Paths, One Light 155
38. Meet Your Five Gurus 160
39. What's Your Next First 166
40. Smile: Life's Emotional Protein 170
41. The Happiest Man on Earth 174
42. Trust in Google, but Don't Forget Your Gut 178
43. The Green Path Behind You 182
44. Junoon: Be Mad Enough to Succeed 187
45. The Weight of Doubt 192

Part 8: Time, Love & What Truly Remains

46. Before the World Wakes Up 199

47. When You Believe, Things Move 203
48. The Hand on the Shoulder 208
49. Call Me When Free... 212
50. Why I Run a Little Faster 216
51. The River That Never Runs Dry 220
52. The Things Worth Bringing Back 224

Part 9: My Top 10 Rules for Professionals

Acknowledgements 234

OFFICE OF GURUDEV SRI SRI RAVI SHANKAR
ART OF LIVING INTERNATIONAL CENTRE, 21 KM KANAKAPURA ROAD,
UDAYPURA, BANGALORE - 82, INDIA P +91.80.67262616 F | +91.80.28432833
SECRETARIAT@ARTOFLIVING.ORG | WWW.SRISRI.ORG |
WWW.ARTOFLIVING.ORG

January 18, 2026

MESSAGE

Human life is precious, yet in the race for external success and recognition, we often lose touch with the true source of fulfillment. It is commendable that the author invites readers to pause, reflect and cultivate self-awareness and responsibility.

I hope that readers will move beyond intellectual understanding and come to experience wisdom not merely at a conceptual level, but as a living reality. This naturally unfolds through meditation. Knowledge cleanses the mind just as soap cleans the body, but then, it is to be rinsed away. Meditation is the immersion in which the mind grows clear, the heart softens and right action arises effortlessly. This is the foundation of a just, prosperous, and joyful society. May this work, in its own way, help to nurture such a world.

Love and Blessings,
Gurudev Sri Sri Ravi Shankar

Foreword

I have known Rajneesh-ji in settings where words are chosen the way numbers are chosen, carefully and precisely. In his corporate avatar as the savvy, hard-nosed CFO of Reliance Jio, and in the boardroom where I served alongside him for 10 years, I admired his mastery over details, his rigorous thought process, and his ability to focus on what mattered.

That is why this book surprised me, in the best possible way.

In these pages, you see a different avatar of Rajneesh. Not a different person, but a fuller one. A man who watches life the way he watches a balance sheet, noticing the small line items that everyone else ignores, and then showing you how those line items quietly determine the outcome. He disarms you with humility, saying he considers himself "an ordinary man" and that his story is "a tribute" to the 99% who build quiet, meaningful lives away from the limelight. That phrase, how to build a quiet, meaningful love, is the soul of this book.

Rajneesh's gift is that he takes small behaviours, the ones we ignore or dismiss as trivial, and reveals the big life lessons hiding inside them.

Take the "₹10 lesson." Two travellers stop for juice. The vendor quotes a fair price. The bargaining begins, as it so often does, not because the buyer cannot pay, but because the buyer can bargain. And then the vendor asks a simple question: "Sir… would you bargain like this for a can of Coke or Pepsi?" That question lands like a quiet verdict. Rajneesh responds by paying more, not less: "₹10 extra, for the lesson."

In that one moment, he exposes an uncomfortable moral asymmetry we all participate in, squeezing those who have the least while paying full price without blinking in air-conditioned stores. He then states the lesson with clarity that makes you pause: "Paying full price to someone who struggles to earn it is not charity, it's humanity."

When people hear "mindfulness," they often imagine a retreat, a quiet room, a special practice, something set apart from ordinary life. Rajneesh's version is simpler and more useful. For him, mindfulness is presence in motion, the ability to see the bigger picture in the smallest moment.

In "Where Are You Going So Fast?", he describes watching a car race past him, the driver wearing the smug grin of victory, only to be trapped minutes later behind a garbage truck, frustrated at life's refusal to cooperate. And then comes the question that should haunt every modern professional: "Where exactly are we all going so fast?"

But the line that stayed with me comes later, in a different scene, a grocery store line, an older man moving slowly, and Rajneesh's piercing lesson: "Maybe he wasn't slow. We were too fast."

That one sentence is a complete philosophy. It reframes the world without blaming it. It makes you ask whether your impatience is really efficiency, or inner turbulence wearing a productivity costume.

Another set of small things Rajneesh-ji focuses on are small inner movements: the assumptions you make, the suspicions you nurture, the fears that quietly shrink your life. In "Letting Go of Fear," he grounds courage not in heroic gestures, but in everyday choices, rarely dramatic and often invisible. Then he offers a very practical definition of courage: choosing "transparency over suspicion," "clarity over gossip," "simplicity over show," and "trust at least once more."

Rajneesh weaves scripture, sages, and poets into his life lessons. He quotes Tagore, reminding us of a mind "without fear and the head held high." But he does not leave Tagore on a pedestal. He uses the poem to offer a practical lesson: "Tomorrow, do one small thing that weakens fear and strengthens trust..."

I love how relational this book is. Rajneesh writes as a leader, yes, but also as a family man, a friend, a student of people, and someone who understands that the best parts of us are often awakened by the gentleness of someone else. In "The Hand on the Shoulder," a senior leader places a hand on his shoulder at a critical moment and says, "When your hand is there, I feel I can take on the world." It is a deceptively small gesture, yet it captures a profound truth about how we lift other people up.

I also love the method that Rajneesh follows in the book. He tells a story, extracts the essence, and then leaves you with an actionable behavioural nudge. This is why the book feels like a necklace of gems rather than a lecture. You can pick up one gem a day. You can wear it immediately. And if you dive deeper, you can adorn your life with a necklace made from these gems.

In a world of targets, projects, and quarterly KPIs, we believe that big outcomes require only big actions. Rajneesh gently dismantles that myth. He shows how small acts compound, morally and emotionally, perhaps a lesson he has learned from financial investing. A ₹10 decision becomes a lesson in dignity. A moment of impatience becomes a diagnosis of our speed addiction. A small act of trust becomes a way to reclaim your humanity. And a hand on a shoulder becomes the quiet architecture of courage.

That, to me, is quiet excellence.

Do not rush as you read this book. Read slowly. Let each reflection settle. And when Rajneesh says "Tomorrow," take him seriously. In a world obsessed with transformation, this book offers something rarer: honest, lived wisdom you can practice in the next five minutes.

Mohanbir Sawhney
McCormick Foundation Professor of Technology
Director, Center for Research in Technology & Innovation
Northwestern Kellogg School of Management

Introduction

It is a privilege to present *Quiet Excellence*, an insightful compilation of 52 life stories authored by CMA Rajneesh Jain, President & CFO, Reliance Jio Infocomm Limited and an eminent member of the profession, who also currently serves as the Chair of the FICCI CFO Council. This publication represents a valuable contribution to professional thought leadership and reflects the depth of experience, wisdom and ethical grounding that the author brings to the finance and governance landscape.

At a time when professional success is often measured in immediacy and visibility, this book draws attention to the enduring principles of quiet excellence like integrity, consistency, thoughtful leadership and purpose-driven decision-making. The author's reflections are drawn from a distinguished career spanning multiple roles and responsibilities, offering readers perspectives that integrate professional rigor with personal values.

The strength of this work lies in its authenticity and relevance. The themes explored go beyond technical expertise to address the human dimensions of leadership, responsibility and faith in one's convictions. These reflections will resonate with professionals across generations, encouraging both introspection and action in an increasingly complex business environment.

The Institute commends the author for this meaningful addition to professional literature. The work strongly aligns with the Institute's core values of excellence, integrity, continuous learning and service to society. It is expected that this book will serve not only as a source of professional guidance, but also as a companion for personal reflection.

This publication is recommended to members of the profession, aspiring leaders and all readers seeking depth, balance and perspective in their professional and personal lives.

Jai Hind!

Srinivasa Prasad, CMA TCA
President, ICMAI

Praise for the Book

At NSE, we have always believed that strong markets are built on strong institutions, and strong institutions are built on values.

Governance, transparency, accountability, and ethical conduct are not just regulatory requirements, they are the foundations of sustainable growth and trust. As India progresses towards becoming a developed economy, the focus must remain not only on growth in numbers, but also on growth in quality, of leadership, culture, and behaviour.

In that context, this book is a timely and important contribution. It reinforces a simple but powerful truth: performance and values are not competing priorities. When organisations embed the right behaviours, customer focus, integrity, ownership, collaboration, and excellence, results follow in a way that is repeatable, resilient, and scalable.

What I appreciate particularly about this work is its practical orientation. It does not treat values as abstract ideals, but as everyday decisions that shape how teams operate, how leaders lead, and how organisations respond under pressure. In today's environment, where businesses face rapid technological change, evolving stakeholder expectations, and heightened scrutiny, culture becomes a competitive advantage.

Companies that build trust internally and externally are better positioned to attract talent, earn customer loyalty, and sustain investor confidence.

I hope this book encourages leaders and professionals across sectors to reflect on the kind of institutions they want to build and the legacy they want to leave behind. India's next phase of growth will be defined not only by the scale of our enterprises, but by the strength of their character.

Ashishkumar Chauhan
Managing Director & CEO
National Stock Exchange of India Limited (NSE)

Praise for the Book

Over the years, Brother Rajneesh's association with the Brahma Kumaris organisation, along with his visits and interactions with senior members of the spiritual community, has supported his exploration of values such as self-awareness, discipline, and purpose-driven living. These influences are not expressed overtly but are quietly visible in the way he approaches work, leadership, and human relationships.

Quiet Excellence is not merely a book for professionals or leaders in organisations. Through simple, thoughtful reflections drawn from lived experience, it speaks to anyone seeking clarity in thought, balance in action, and meaning in everyday life. The book gently reminds the reader that outer success finds its true strength when rooted in inner stability, ethical conduct, and conscious decision-making.

We believe these reflections will resonate with readers who aspire to live and work with greater awareness, responsibility, and purpose. May this book serve as a companion for those who seek to harmonise professional excellence with inner growth.

With good wishes,
In Service of Humanity

BK Asha
Member, Management Committee,
Brahma Kumaris, Mount Abu
Director, Om Shanti Retreat Centre, Gurugram
Director, BK Centres of Delhi Zone

Preface

When the idea of sharing my life story came up, I hesitated. The big biographies were for the giants—people like Ratan Tata, Mahatma Gandhi, individuals whose lives seemed etched in significance from the start.

The power to influence lies with celebrities, who are paid handsomely to promote ideas and products. A single word or emoticon posted by a star sends the entire social media network into a tizzy!

But think about it. Celebrities form less than 1% of our population. All around us, ordinary people are doing ordinary things that offer us incredible lessons in the art of living. Perhaps there is beauty, even inspiration, in capturing that every day journey.

I, too, consider myself an ordinary man, born into an ordinary family. My own story is hardly significant enough to fill the pages of a book. But I take immense pride in being among 99% of the ordinary ones who hustle every day, building quiet, meaningful lives away from the limelight.

My story is a tribute to the everyday courage it takes to face life, to be resilient in the face of small challenges and heartbreaks, and to find meaning even when it isn't easily visible. It's about showing up, again and again, ready to face whatever life throws your way. And perhaps, in telling this story, I hope to honour the journey of every ordinary person whose life is woven with grit, small victories, and a quiet, enduring hope.

Rajneesh Jain

PART 1

The Little Things That Change Everything

1

The Big Deal That Cost Just ₹10

A few years ago, on the way to Shri Kedarnath, my friend and I stopped at a tiny roadside stall selling fresh bel (wood apple) juice. If you've travelled in the hills, you've probably seen one — steel glasses stacked in a neat pyramid, a small wooden bench, and a vendor whose smile feels warmer than the sunlight. The drink was delicious, perfectly cold, and exactly what we needed after a long and tiring climb.

When we finished, we casually asked the price.

"Hundred rupees, sir," the vendor said.

Before I could respond, my friend jumped in. "Arrey bhai, that's too much! We'll give you eighty."

It was the kind of bargaining we do without thinking. Almost automatic.

The vendor didn't argue. He simply smiled and asked one question:

"Sir… would you bargain like this for a can of Coke or Pepsi?"

Those words lingered in the air. There was no anger, no sarcasm — just a quiet truth. My friend fell silent. I reached into my pocket, pulled out ₹110, handed it to the vendor, and said, "₹10 extra — for the lesson."

As we walked away, my friend murmured, "He's right... we would never bargain at a supermarket." And he was right — we don't. We pay the printed price without hesitation. Somehow, the rules of fairness seem to change when the shop has a tin roof and a dirt floor.

That moment has stayed with me far longer than the taste of that bel juice. I've often thought about how quickly we negotiate with people who work the hardest for their money, and how easily we swipe our cards in air-conditioned stores without a second thought. The contrast is uncomfortable. Those with the least bargaining power are often the ones we bargain with the most.

Over time, I began noticing other moments like this — the vegetable vendor who agrees to a ₹10 reduction with a tired smile, the rickshaw driver who doesn't argue even when we underpay, the cobbler who hasn't changed his rates in years yet still gets questioned. We tell ourselves, "It's normal to bargain..." It's part of the culture. But is it always fair?

The truth is, saving ten or twenty rupees rarely changes our day. But for someone earning just enough to get by, that amount could mean a meal, a school notebook, or simply a sense of dignity.

That day in Kedarnath taught me something simple: generosity doesn't always require grand gestures. Sometimes it's just about not taking away from someone who already has very little. Paying the full price to someone who struggles to earn it is not charity — it is basic humanity.

So once in a while, if you can, choose not to bargain. If the price feels reasonable, pay it. Maybe even add a little extra. Sometimes, ten rupees can teach you more than a thousand-rupee workshop on empathy.

We bargain because we can. But maybe, once in a while, we should pause and ask: should we?

₹10 for a million-dollar lesson. Truly the best deal of my life.

The Core Idea

Tomorrow, resist the instinct to bargain with a small vendor. Pay the price they quote — perhaps even a little more. Notice how it feels to choose kindness over saving a few rupees.

2

The Puppy Who Taught Me About Anger Management

More than three decades ago, a colleague of mine walked into the office looking unusually quiet. Not sad, not angry — just weighed down. When I asked him what was wrong, he sighed and said, "I feel terrible about my puppy." That caught my attention immediately. He then told me a story that has stayed with me ever since.

The previous day, his boss had scolded him in a meeting. The words were harsh, and they were spoken in front of everyone. He came home feeling hurt and humiliated. Wanting a moment of comfort, he asked his wife for a cup of tea. Seeing him sweaty and upset, she gently suggested, "Why don't you take a bath first?"

In that moment, the smallest spark was enough. He snapped. Sharp words, raised voice — the works. She said nothing. But anger doesn't disappear. It moves.

A little later, while helping her nine-year-old son with his homework, she noticed a small mistake — something she would normally have ignored. But the leftover anger needed somewhere to go. The boy was scolded far more than he deserved. He burst into tears.

And then came the last link in the chain. The family puppy, who toddled over to comfort the crying child, was pushed away in frustration. The little creature, confused and hurt, crawled into a corner. And that is where the "anger chain" stopped — because he was the only one who had no one else to pass his pain on to.

My colleague told me this with genuine remorse. That image — the puppy curled up silently — haunted him. And honestly, it stayed with me too. It made me realise something simple but powerful: most of us don't remove stress. We transfer it. Like a parcel passed from one person to another until it reaches someone too small or too powerless to pass it further.

And the tragic part is this: the person who suffers most often had nothing to do with the original problem.

After that day, I made a quiet promise to myself. When anger shows up — and it will, because we are human — I must try to stop it with me. Not hand it over to the next unsuspecting person who crosses my path.

It is not easy. But it is possible.

I realised that a few small habits make a big difference. The first is recognising the exact moment when stress tries to jump from your chest into your voice. If you can catch that second, half the battle is won. Reacting feels natural. Pausing takes strength. But that pause can change everything.

I also learnt the value of stepping away. Walking to a window. Drinking a glass of water. Sitting quietly for a few minutes. Letting the body cool down so the mind can follow. It is surprising how often anger fades simply because you did not feed it.

Another powerful practice is sharing. Not shouting, not blaming — just honestly saying, "I had a rough day. I feel upset." The moment you express it calmly, the anger softens. It becomes something you can handle together instead of something you throw at someone else.

Helping someone else works almost like magic. It sounds strange, but when you are upset and choose to be kind to someone, your emotional state shifts. It is difficult to stay angry while doing something genuinely good.

And above all, never let revenge settle in your mind. It does not punish the other person; it quietly harms you. Vent if you must — but vent safely. Imagine speaking to a temporary version of that person in your mind. Say what you need to say, and then let it go. That is far better than hurting someone who does not deserve it.

That day taught me something no book ever did: anger usually travels downward. And unless someone consciously stops it, someone innocent gets hurt. Sometimes it is a spouse. Sometimes a child. Sometimes a pet. Sometimes even your own health.

We cannot always control who hurts us. But we can control who we hurt next.

The Core Idea

Tomorrow, when something angers or frustrates you, pause for ten seconds before reacting. Do not pass the stress forward. Break the chain right there. One moment of awareness can prevent hurt, protect relationships, and keep the "puppy" in your life safe.

3

Keep Shining Anyway

I've been walking up Parsik Hill in Navi Mumbai for almost twenty years now. Same path, same trees, the same breeze that somehow feels different each season. And every time I climb, my eyes automatically drift upward to one thing — a beautiful snow-white bungalow perched right at the top. It stands there gracefully, catching the sunlight at just the right angle, instantly lifting my mood. I don't know who lives there, but it has always made the climb feel worthwhile.

Then one year, a tall, boxy tower came up right in front of it. Almost overnight, the bungalow disappeared from view. Hidden. Overshadowed. Blocked by a structure with no charm, no poetry — just height.

I remember feeling unexpectedly disappointed. How could something so beautiful vanish so easily? Something that had stood there for decades, quietly admired by so many walkers like me?

But that is life.

You can be doing everything right. You can be consistent, sincere, talented — even exceptional — and still get overshadowed by someone newer, louder, or simply better placed. A new hire grabs the spotlight. A younger colleague becomes the boss's favourite. A trend replaces years of expertise. A fast talker overshadows your slow, steady work.

Suddenly, you are no longer visible.

Not because you stopped shining. But because something else stood in front of you.

At first, it feels unfair. It feels personal. It feels as if the world has moved on without you. But visibility is seasonal. And sometimes, invisibility is preparation.

A few years after the tower blocked that bungalow, a meditation centre — Dhamma Vipula — came up at the edge of Parsik Hill. A proper road was built. More people began climbing. And just like that, the angle changed. The snow-white bungalow became visible again — clearer than before — as if it had simply waited for the right moment.

That day, standing there with the wind against my face, I felt as if life was quietly teaching me something: angles change.

When someone else's shadow dims your presence, you don't always need to fight it. You don't need to rush back into the light or prove yourself constantly. You just need to keep doing the work — steadily, sincerely, without depending on applause.

Because new roads do get built. Circumstances shift. The world rearranges itself. And those who stay committed eventually come back into view, often with more depth and dignity than before.

I've seen this in organisations as well. When new projects begin or businesses diversify, the people who once seemed to fade into the background suddenly become essential again. Their experience, maturity, and steadiness — once overlooked — turn into their biggest strengths.

A diamond does not lose its value because it is covered in mud. It simply waits to be uncovered. And sometimes, you are the one who must keep polishing yourself quietly.

While thinking about all this, I once came across a story about the author Todd Henry. In a business meeting, a speaker asked, "Where is the richest land in the world?" People answered — the Gulf, Africa, diamond mines, oil fields.

But the speaker said, "No. It is the cemetery."

The cemetery is the richest place on earth because it holds ideas never executed, books never written, inventions never created, music never composed, words never spoken, kindness never expressed. Lives full of potential that never reached the world.

That thought stayed with me.

Henry later wrote his book *Die Empty*, built around that idea: don't leave this world with your best still inside you.

We spend so much energy trying to be visible. Trying to be appreciated. Trying to stay relevant. But maybe the real question is not, "Am I being noticed?" Instead, it is, "Am I giving my best?" Is my potential reaching others, or is it waiting inside me for a perfect moment that may never come?

Whether the world applauds or not, you deserve to live in a way that does not bury your gifts with you.

Imagine carrying your creativity, insights, and generosity through life — only for all of it to remain unused. That would be the real loss.

So here is the reminder: visibility fades. Contribution stays.

Some of the greatest impact-makers were invisible in their own time. Some of the kindest acts are never recorded. Some of the most meaningful work happens quietly, long before recognition arrives.

Your job is not to be seen every day. Your job is to keep shining every day — whether someone is watching or not. Because life keeps building new roads. New angles appear. And when they do, those who remained steady are the ones who stand out.

Just like that snow-white bungalow on Parsik Hill — patient, beautiful, and ready when the view opened again.

The Core Idea

Tomorrow, do one thing you've been postponing simply because no one will notice it — write one page, make one call, help one person, finish one pending task. Visibility may come later. Contribution begins now.

4

The Keys to a Happy Life

We spend much of our lives chasing happiness as if it's a prize waiting at the finish line — the right job, the right house, the right bank balance, the right number of holidays each year. But over time, you realise something quietly profound: happiness doesn't arrive ready-made. It has to be built, brick by brick, through small, almost invisible choices.

I understood this more deeply when an old colleague visited me after many years. He had always been ambitious — airport lounges, five-star meetings, 14-hour workdays, constant upgrades. That day, he stood in my living room thinner than I remembered, slightly worn around the edges. "I spent my youth building a life," he said, "but forgot to build a life I could enjoy." His health had declined, his temper had shortened, and loneliness had slowly crept in.

As we sat over tea and he spoke about sleepless nights and sudden health scares, something became very clear to me: the real keys to a happy life are surprisingly simple. We ignore them because they are quiet. They don't trend. They don't demand attention. They just quietly work.

Health is a perfect example. A friend once joked, "Why buy insurance when hospitals are the only ones who benefit?" But the truth is, no insurance policy can buy good health. No document can restore the freshness of a morning walk or the strength in your legs. That responsibility is yours alone. You can outsource almost everything in life — but not your well-being.

Happiness works in the same way. Pleasure is easy — a dessert, a new phone, a holiday. Pleasure can be purchased. Happiness cannot. It is built internally. It comes from choosing the right company, creating a healthy mental environment, and learning to let go of small, petty irritations that crowd your mind.

Avoid unpleasant surroundings — whether people or places. Negativity spreads quickly, and sometimes the bravest thing you can do is quietly step away from what drains you. In fact, I would urge you to write this somewhere you can see it daily: *Do yourself a favour. Step away from negativity. Your life will change.*

I once met a retired banker who shared a simple piece of wisdom about ageing: "Save money so you can afford dignity." That line stayed with me. Dependency quietly steals happiness. When you are financially stable — even modestly — you give yourself freedom. The freedom to choose, to move, to say no, and to sleep peacefully.

And while we're speaking of ageing, there is no rule that says you must "act" your age. Dress well. Feel young. Look after yourself. You are not trying to impress anyone; you are honouring your own spirit. A crisp shirt or a well-chosen saree can lift your confidence more than any motivational talk.

Another underrated key is humour. Spend time with people who make you laugh — really laugh. The kind of laughter that washes away the bitterness of a tough day. Humour is medicine without side effects. A good laugh can reset your mood faster than anything else.

Music, too, becomes a quiet companion as the years pass. When children move out, when friends grow fewer, when the house feels too silent, music keeps the heart open. A familiar song can gently carry you from sadness to comfort within minutes.

Energy is another key — the inner fire that refuses to fade. Call it drive, willpower, or hunger. I am speaking about the spark of latent energy within you. People begin to lose happiness when they stop wanting to learn, grow, or try something new. There is no age limit on curiosity. I've seen 70-year-olds take up yoga, 60-year-olds start painting, and 50-year-olds begin new careers. In fact, those years often bring the freedom to try what you could not in your youth. There is deep joy in staying mentally alive.

And perhaps the most beautiful advice of all: treasure only the pleasant moments. The unpleasant ones will come — of course they will — but don't store them. We are not snakes; we don't need to carry venom for later use. Let the wrongs go. Let the hurts go. Let the grudges go. Holding on only poisons your inner world. Happiness needs space. Remove the clutter.

When you look closely, life is not demanding grand achievements from us. It is asking for balance. A happy person is not someone without problems, but someone who knows when to pause, when to breathe, when to laugh, when to save, when to walk away, when to begin again, when to forgive, and when to simply enjoy the sunlight on their face.

Happiness is not hidden. It is waiting to be chosen — one small action at a time.

The Core Idea

Tomorrow, pick one simple happiness habit and practise it deliberately: take a 20-minute walk, call someone who makes you laugh, declutter one corner of your home, or eat your meal without a screen. Happiness grows when nurtured daily — like sunlight slowly filling a room.

5

The Mess We Make

During my morning walk at Parsik Hill one day, I saw a large group from one of the biggest NGOs in the world sweeping the paths, clearing plastic bottles from bushes, and packing piles of discarded snack packets into large black bags. It was a genuine effort — sincere volunteers, clear signage, visible enthusiasm — the kind of initiative that makes you feel hopeful, at least for a while.

But as I looked around, one uncomfortable thought surfaced: Is this enough?

Because by tomorrow morning, Parsik Hill will likely look the same again. Fresh paan stains on the walls. New gutka wrappers on the railings. Crushed tetra packs kicked into bushes. Beer cans rolling lazily near the track. Dog poop sitting squarely in the middle of the walking path. Someone blowing their nose and leaving the tissue behind as a silent signature.

The sad truth is that clean-up drives work only for a few hours. What defeats them is not a lack of effort — but a lack of fear. A lack of accountability. A deep-rooted belief that someone else will clean up after us.

And the incorrigible ones? They will probably laugh and say, "Arre, kal phir ganda kar denge."

The only real way to change deeply ingrained habits is through something many of us may not like — but absolutely need: strict, consistent rules that pinch the pocket and disturb comfort.

I have seen this work beautifully in other countries. In Singapore, if you casually flick a cigarette butt onto the ground, chances are an officer will appear before the butt stops rolling. The system works because littering carries heavy fines. Someone fined once rarely repeats the mistake — not there, not anywhere.

Even in India, we've seen how enforcement and technology can transform behaviour. In some cities, you jump a red light and the fine reaches your WhatsApp before you reach home. It stays on your record, quietly affecting renewals and insurance. Suddenly, the rule people once mocked becomes a rule they respect.

During the pandemic, masks at Marine Drive were compulsory. Volunteers photographed those who broke the rule, making arguments pointless. People complained, yes — but they complied. Because real-time enforcement works.

The point is simple: awareness alone does not change behaviour. Awareness plus accountability does.

We already have enough campaigns. What we need now is consistent, technology-backed enforcement supported by NGOs and municipal teams — working together as one system.

Imagine a practical, enforceable model rolled out nationwide:

- Ban smoking, drinking, or eating in public spaces unless clearly designated and equipped with disposal bins.
- Make poop collectors for pet owners non-negotiable.
- Hold food vendors responsible for keeping a 10-foot radius clean — or fine them.
- Install CCTV cameras that are actually connected to automated penalty systems, not just decorative fixtures.
- Impose higher fines for repeat offenders, or temporary suspension of certain civic privileges where legally feasible.

None of this is impossible. It requires consistency — small, daily enforcement that gradually rewires public behaviour.

Here is the uncomfortable truth: a society that faces consequences behaves better than one that relies only on appeals to conscience.

We proudly say, "Japan is so clean." But Japan became clean because cleanliness became discipline.

We admire Singapore's spotless streets but forget that their standards are the result of decades of firm enforcement.

India has the heart. India has the manpower. India has the technology. What we sometimes lack is the resolve to enforce rules uniformly — without favour, without turning away, without saying, "Yeh toh chalta hai."

And yet, I remain hopeful.

When I see schoolchildren put wrappers into their bags because teachers insist on it... when housing societies quietly implement segregation... when one person asks another not to litter... I realise change has already begun. It is just slower than we would like.

Prevention is always better than cure. That is true for personal health — and just as true for the health of a nation.

If we want a cleaner India, we need fewer symbolic clean-up drives and more consistent prevention.

The Core Idea

Tomorrow, take one simple step: carry a small pouch in your pocket or bag for dry waste — wrappers, receipts, tissues. Do not throw anything on the road, even if there is no bin nearby. Start with yourself. One small habit, practised consistently, can influence the people around you more than any campaign. Because a cleaner India will not begin with a broom. It will begin with a choice.

6

A Pinch of Spice

The other day, I saw a dear friend standing happily at a roadside thela, enjoying chaat with the kind of enthusiasm usually reserved for five-star buffets. I teased him, "Yaar, you? Here? I thought you only ate in places where the water comes in glass bottles." He laughed, wiped his hands on a tissue, and said, "Boss, once in a while, you need the thela experience. Thoda masala chahiye life mein!"

I knew exactly what he meant.

A few days later, my wife and I were buying vegetables. After everything was packed, she began her favourite ritual — bargaining. For fifteen minutes she negotiated warmly with the vendor, both of them smiling, both fully aware that the grand saving of the day would be... fifty rupees. When we finally walked away, I asked, "Was that really worth all that time?" She looked at me as if I had completely missed the point. "Arey, if there's no bargaining, where's the fun in shopping? Thoda tadka toh banta hai!"

And she was right. Not every joy in life comes from efficiency.

At work, I once met a colleague who looked unusually dull. This was not his usual animated self, so I asked what happened. He sighed, "Sir, my boss hasn't shouted at me in two weeks." For a moment I thought he was joking. After all, he had often complained about the boss's temper. But now he missed the drama. "I'm used to it," he admitted. "Life feels flat without that spark."

I couldn't help but smile. Human beings are strange. We think we want complete calm, but too much calm begins to feel like plain khichdi — healthy, yes, but where's the excitement?

Even in public speaking, storytellers who add humour, exaggeration, quirks, and emotional twists often hold our attention more than those who stick strictly to facts. It's not that facts are unimportant — they are. But our minds respond to flavour. A story with the right masala stays with us long after it ends.

Perhaps that's why you'll often see an elderly uncle in his 80s cracking jokes, gossiping cheerfully, or bargaining over coriander leaves with the energy of a teenager. Age may slow the body, but it rarely dulls the appetite for life's tadka. A little banter here, a little drama there — we thrive on these small bursts of colour.

The truth is, most days follow a predictable rhythm — wake up, work, eat, repeat. Without small detours, playful exchanges, harmless indulgences, and unexpected moments of laughter or even irritation, life can begin to feel like a long corridor with no windows. The spice of life is not about inviting chaos. It is about welcoming variety. It is about allowing small surprises to brighten an otherwise orderly day.

Think about the stories you remember most. They are rarely about days when everything went perfectly. They are about moments when something amusing happened, when plans changed, when someone said something unexpected, when you tried something new. Those are the memories that stay.

Life doesn't need a dramatic makeover to feel meaningful. Sometimes it just needs a pinch of masala — a quirky conversation, a new food stall, a playful argument over prices, a harmless office tamasha that breaks the routine.

So the next time a friend drags you to a roadside vendor, or someone insists on bargaining for coriander, or you find yourself in the middle of light-hearted drama at work, smile. These little spices are what keep life interesting.

A perfectly calm life may sound ideal. But a life with flavour? That is unforgettable.

The Core Idea

Tomorrow, deliberately add one small pinch of masala to your day — try a new food, take a different route, talk to someone unexpected, or welcome a small unscripted moment. Life does not need to be perfect. It just needs a little flavour.

7

Letting Go of Fear

A few weeks ago, while I was walking on the left side of the road — as per norms — my friend tugged at my arm and said, "Yaar, walk on the right. At least you'll see the cars coming. On the left, they can hit you from behind."

His tone was casual. The implication wasn't.

It made me pause. Is this what life has become? Looking over our shoulders, expecting to be hit from behind? Waiting for an unexpected blow — on the road, at work, even in relationships?

How can the mind be free of fear when mistrust has quietly turned into a survival skill?

Today, we repeat phrases like punchlines:

"In God we trust, all others must bring data."

It sounds clever. But beneath the humour lies deep suspicion.

There's also that corporate joke: "Show me the man, and I'll show you the rule." Somewhere along the way, we began believing that rules are not universal — they depend on who is standing in front of us.

We applaud polished presentations without checking if the work behind them is solid. Appearance often overshadows substance. Even in personal relationships, people admit — sometimes lightly, sometimes seriously — that you can't be too open. The same person you trust today may stand against you tomorrow.

It is exhausting to live like this — with the mind constantly alert, scanning for danger like a security system that never switches off.

And yet, every now and then, something softens that fear.

Something reminds you that caution is not the only way to survive.

A few years ago, someone told me, "I live by one simple rule: Assume good intent unless proven otherwise."

I laughed. "Isn't that risky?"

He smiled. "So is assuming the worst."

He was right. Fear can protect you at times. But it also builds walls — walls so high that nothing nourishing can enter.

Over the years, I've met people who operate from this quiet courage. A colleague who trained his team so well that they eventually outperformed him — and he celebrated it. A friend who lent money to someone who had once wronged him, because he believed in second chances. Their decisions were not driven by fear.

And on days when fear feels heavy, I think of Tagore.

When Rabindranath Tagore wrote *Where the mind is without fear*, he envisioned a nation awake in thought, free in conscience, brave in truth. More than a century later, his words feel surprisingly current.

Where the mind is without fear and the head is held high
Where knowledge is free
Where the world has not been broken up into fragments…

How easily our world breaks into fragments today — work versus home, mine versus yours, community versus community, even WhatsApp group versus WhatsApp group. And in that fragmentation, fear quietly finds space to grow.

"Into that heaven of freedom, my Father, let my country awake," Tagore prayed.

I sometimes wonder what that heaven of freedom looks like in daily life.

Perhaps it looks like speaking honestly in a meeting, even if your view is unpopular.

Perhaps it looks like trusting a colleague with responsibility instead of micromanaging out of insecurity.

Perhaps it looks like allowing your child to make mistakes instead of shielding them from every discomfort.

Perhaps it even looks like walking on the road without constantly expecting to be hit from behind — literally and metaphorically.

Courage, I have learned, is rarely dramatic. It is not about grand heroics. It is about small, steady choices — choosing transparency over suspicion, clarity over gossip, simplicity over show, trust at least once more, even after disappointment.

It is not easy.

But neither is living in constant fear.

I do not know when our country will fully reflect Tagore's dream. But each of us can move a little closer to it. Freedom of the mind is not a national event. It is a personal practice.

The Core Idea

Tomorrow, do one small thing that weakens fear and strengthens trust — send a message you've been postponing, tell someone the truth kindly, admit a mistake, forgive a minor irritation, or simply choose to believe that someone's intention is good. Fear may keep you cautious. But trust — when given wisely — keeps you human.

PART 2

Work, Leadership & Quiet Grace

8

The Leader as Teacher

There's an old story I heard years ago, but it has stayed with me like a gentle hand on the shoulder. A young man once ran into his school teacher after many years. They exchanged the usual smiles and pleasantries, but then the former student hesitated. Something inside him wanted to confess a secret he had carried since childhood.

"Sir," he said quietly, "do you remember the day someone stole a watch in class?"

The teacher nodded.

"That was me," the man continued. "I was terrified that day. You asked all of us to stand in a line and close our eyes while you searched our pockets. I was certain my school life was over. But you never took my name. You never exposed me. You saved me from humiliation. Whatever I became later… it began with that kindness."

The teacher smiled gently and replied with something the man never expected.

"I had closed my eyes too," he said. "So that even I wouldn't know who the child was."

That line struck me more deeply than any management book ever has. *I had closed my eyes too.* The teacher understood something we often forget: people may remember punishment, but they are transformed by grace.

I have seen versions of this story play out in professional life as well. In one of my early jobs, a young employee made a mistake that could easily have turned into a disciplinary issue. Nothing illegal or dramatic — just the kind of mistake people make when they are still learning. I remember the fear on his face when he entered my office, convinced his career had ended before it had properly begun.

But something in me said: correct him, don't crush him.

We discussed it, corrected what could be corrected, and moved forward. Years later, he told me that this single moment changed how he viewed himself at work.

Leadership is not always about bold strategies or high-stakes decisions. Often, it is about quiet choices: whether to shame or support, whether to expose or protect, whether to break confidence or build it. A good leader does more than manage tasks; he shapes people.

Over time, I've realised that leaders tend to fall into three broad types.

First, there is the leader of the masses — the one who may not be the deepest technical expert but has a remarkable ability to rally people, resolve conflict, and convert scattered effort into unified action. These leaders are like orchestra conductors. They may not play every instrument, but they bring out the best in each player. They thrive amid complexity and hold teams together under pressure.

Second, there is the expert leader — someone who has mastered a field so thoroughly that others naturally seek their direction. These leaders know their craft inside out. Their authority comes from competence. They set standards, maintain quality, and act as steady anchors when uncertainty rises.

And then there are consultant-leaders — the thinkers, storytellers, and strategists. They shape perspectives. They frame problems clearly and illuminate possibilities. They often operate close to senior leadership, influencing decisions not through hierarchy, but through insight.

None of these types is superior to the others. Problems arise only when people are pushed into roles that do not align with their natural strengths. I have seen brilliant experts struggle in people-management roles they did not enjoy. I have seen inspiring mass-leaders trapped in narrow specialist roles that drained their energy. And I have seen natural strategists told to "just execute," slowly losing their spark.

A fulfilling career begins with understanding your own strengths.

The teacher in the watch story was not powerful because of authority. He was powerful because of empathy. That is why his student carried that memory into adulthood.

Leadership truly begins the day you choose to lift someone instead of breaking them.

If there is one lesson I've learnt over decades, it is this: people rarely remember your targets, deadlines, or achievements. But they always remember how you made them feel in their most vulnerable moments. They remember whose eyes were closed when they made a mistake.

The Core Idea

Tomorrow, before reacting, pause for three seconds. That tiny pause is where teaching begins — and judgement ends.

9

The 5% Club

There is something about the early years of your career that never leaves you. The energy. The nervousness. The constant desire to prove yourself. It is like carrying a restless engine inside you that keeps you moving.

I was in that phase when I found myself handling the Accounts Payable function. It sounds simple, almost dull — until you picture the mountain of paperwork we dealt with in those pre-email, pre-ERP days. Real letters. Real stamps. Real vendor representatives waiting outside your office with very real irritation on their faces.

Every morning, my desk looked like a post office counter during Diwali. Letters, reminders, complaints — all pointing to one thing: delayed payments. As a young manager who believed every complaint reflected personal failure, I felt constantly overwhelmed. Why were so many people upset? Why were so many bills pending? Why did I feel like the villain in every vendor's story?

One Sunday — a day meant for chai, cricket, and proper rest — I called my team into the office. They arrived curious and slightly anxious. I hadn't told them why, and perhaps that added to the tension.

Then I began opening drawers.

In any office, drawers hide stories. I knew that. But what I found still surprised me. Stacks of old invoices — not lost, not forgotten — just kept aside. Every team member had a pile. And every pile told the same story:

"These were the tricky ones."

"Mismatched amounts."

"Missing signatures."

"Incorrect purchase orders."

"Wrong quantities."

"The ones that required follow-up."

In short, these were not high-volume problems. They were high-effort problems.

My team expected an explosion. Their faces were tense, like students waiting for exam results. But instead of anger, something else clicked in my mind.

I calculated the total value of all the pending "problem bills" across the department. The result was startling. They made up less than 5% of our total monthly billing.

Ninety-five percent of our work was smooth, efficient, and accurate. Yet this unresolved 5% was creating almost all the stress.

That was my turning point.

Our pressure did not come from the 95% we handled well. It came from the 5% we avoided.

That small corner — postponed, ignored, buried in drawers — was responsible for most of the tension in the department. It was the pebble in the shoe. The mosquito in the room. Tiny, but impossible to ignore.

So instead of scolding the team, I did something different. I created what I jokingly called "The 5% Club." I partnered with the sharpest problem-solver on the team, and together we began tackling the pending pile. Vendor by vendor. Issue by issue. A correction here. A phone call there. An amended purchase order. A missing signature. Nothing glamorous — but deeply satisfying.

Within three months, vendor complaints dropped dramatically.

All because we addressed what everyone had been avoiding.

That phase taught me something I still carry with me:

Most people spend their lives polishing the 95%. They celebrate easy wins. They repeat comfortable routines. They improve what is already working. But real growth — personal or professional — hides inside the stubborn, inconvenient 5%.

Think about your own life.

That one health habit you keep postponing.

That one friendship you need to repair.

That one uncomfortable conversation you've avoided.

That one document you never file.

That one habit quietly draining your time.

That one work issue you know needs attention — but you keep delaying.

We all have drawers filled with 5% problems.

And just like in my Accounts Payable office, those ignored corners end up controlling the quality of our days far more than the 95% we manage well.

Over the years, I have seen brilliant teams struggle because no one wanted to touch the difficult 5%. I have seen families carry unnecessary strain because one small issue remained unaddressed. And I have seen organisations grow rapidly when someone finally chose to fix what others preferred to postpone.

Becoming part of the 5% Club is not glamorous. It does not bring immediate applause. It demands patience, humility, and the willingness to deal with messy details.

But it changes you.

There is a special confidence that comes from solving hard problems. A quiet pride. And sometimes, your solution helps not just you, but many others facing the same issue.

Innovation often begins when someone asks, "Why has no one fixed this?" — and then decides to fix it.

The Core Idea

Tomorrow, instead of improving your 95%, identify one lingering "drawer item" — a small but stubborn problem you've been avoiding — and address it. Clean that one corner. Untangle that one knot. You may be surprised at how much lighter the rest of your life feels.

10

BHEL: The First Chapter I Still Revisit

While sorting through some old folders recently, a photograph from 1987 slipped out and stopped me in my tracks. It was our ET Finance batch at BHEL — young faces, crisp shirts, wide smiles, and that unmistakable enthusiasm that only a first job can bring. One glance, and I was transported back to a time that feels like another life, yet still lives quietly within me.

Back then, our three months of training were famously called *Bharat Darshan* — and the name was no exaggeration. We travelled from Trichy to Bhopal, then to Hyderabad, and finally to Haridwar — four major plants, four distinct worlds. Each place had its own rhythm, its own warmth, its own flavour.

At every location, the Learning & Development team was ready with thick manuals, plant visits, sessions with cross-functional heads, and schedules so packed that even our exhaustion felt satisfying.

This wasn't "training" in the modern sense. No online modules. No slideshows. This was immersion. We walked factory floors, stood close enough to feel the hum of machines, watched boilers being assembled piece by piece, and listened to senior engineers explain processes that first seemed intimidating but slowly revealed their logic when you paid attention.

And then there was the other side of Bharat Darshan — the joy of discovering new cities with batchmates. Poha in Bhopal. Dosa in Trichy. Biryani in Hyderabad. Buses, auto-rickshaws, even the occasional cycle ride to visit a temple, a lake, or a bustling market. Our TA/DA felt princely back then, and we stretched every rupee to squeeze in an extra filter coffee or a plate of jalebis. Evenings were filled with laughter, inside jokes, and long conversations about our future — discussions that felt casual then but shaped us more than we realised.

BHEL in those days was a world of its own. The townships were green, peaceful, and self-contained. There was a school, a medical centre, a convention hall screening movies on weekends, playgrounds filled with children, and neighbours who felt like extended family. It was the kind of place where you recognised faces on your evening walk and where festivals were celebrated as if the entire township belonged to one large household.

Professionally too, BHEL was ahead of its time. The manuals were encyclopaedic — thorough, carefully drafted, and deeply practical. Accounting, stores, cash management, processes — answers existed for almost every question. Even today, when I design a process or tackle a bottleneck,

I instinctively reach for the clarity I learned from those manuals.

BHEL was also among the early adopters of accounting automation. They included sections in the Balance Sheet on inflation accounting and even a Social Balance Sheet — concepts most private companies were not thinking about then. Discipline, structure, and routine were woven into the organisation's DNA. The factory hooter would sound, and you knew the shift had begun. It would sound again, and the township seemed to move in quiet rhythm.

The only part that didn't fully suit me was the fixed promotion cycle. Everyone progressed at the same pace — no fast track, no detours. For someone young, restless, and eager to move faster, it felt limiting. After eight unforgettable years, I made the difficult decision to leave.

But I never really left emotionally.

Even today, when someone from my team resigns, I feel the same tug in my chest that I felt when I left BHEL. Recently, a colleague came to meet me on her last day. She spoke about what she had learned, what she had built, the compassion she had experienced, and the dreams she was carrying into her next chapter. She had tears in her eyes. I did too. Because when you build something together over years, it becomes more than work. It becomes family.

We don't talk about this enough. We spend more waking hours at work than at home. If there is no emotional connection — no shared laughter, no shared frustrations, no gentle guidance, no small celebrations — work slowly turns into a burden. And when work feels heavy, everything else begins to feel heavier too.

Sometimes I wonder whether organisations today can recreate the belonging BHEL gave us. A place where you are not just an employee ID, but someone whose children's names people remember. Where a neighbour knocks on your door because they noticed the lights were off. Where competition does not suffocate relationships. Where the pace is steady, learning is deep, and respect flows naturally.

My first job at BHEL Haridwar shaped me more than any qualification ever could. The lush parks, the unhurried evenings, the factory hooter marking the rhythm of the day, the weekly market visits, the community festivals, the modest yet meaningful lifestyle — those years taught me discipline, humility, teamwork, and the value of strong processes.

But above all, they taught me that an organisation is only as strong as the human bonds it nurtures.

You may change cities, companies, titles, or designations. But your first workplace — your first professional "world" — never really leaves you.

The Core Idea

Tomorrow, make one small effort to strengthen the emotional bond at your workplace. Ask a colleague how they truly are. Appreciate someone without a specific reason. Offer help before being asked. When workplaces become more human, work stops feeling like work.

11

Live Like the Coconut Tree

Every time I see a coconut tree, I pause for a moment. It stands tall, steady, almost quiet in its dignity. And yet, it is one of the most useful trees nature has given us. Nothing about it goes to waste — not the water, not the fruit, not the husk, not even the hard shell. Everything has a purpose. Everything contributes. The more I think about it, the more it feels like a beautiful blueprint for how we can shape our own lives and careers.

When we are young, many of us chase the idea of being "successful" — the fruit, the shine, the part that gets photographed and applauded. But the coconut tree gently reminds us that usefulness is far more powerful than glamour. Growth is not only about rising higher; it is about contributing at every stage, in whatever way life needs you. Life doesn't demand perfection. It simply asks us to stay useful, stay grounded, and keep evolving — one stage at a time.

The coconut tree doesn't try to become anything else. It simply gives — and in giving, it becomes invaluable.

Here is how each part of the coconut tree quietly reflects our professional journeys:

Coconut Water — The Early Years

The sweet water inside a tender coconut is refreshing and energising. That is exactly what young professionals are like — full of enthusiasm, freshness, and ideas. They may not have years of experience, but they bring agility and drive. When organisations channel this early energy well, it becomes the fuel that pushes projects forward. Just as coconut water replenishes the body, young talent replenishes the organisation.

Coconut Flesh — Skills That Ripen With Time

As the coconut matures, the tender flesh becomes firm and nourishing. Its uses multiply — you can cook with it, extract oil, turn it into sweets. Our skills evolve in a similar way. Early in our careers, we are still learning. Over time, with experience and study, we become stronger and more versatile. The same person who once struggled with basics eventually handles complex tasks or leads teams. Maturity brings depth.

The Husk — The Team Builder

The fibrous husk is often overlooked, yet it is strong enough to make ropes and mats — things that bind and support. In organisations, these are the seasoned professionals who may not always be in the spotlight, but they hold teams together. They connect people, steady communication, and bring stability. Without them, structures loosen.

The husk reminds us that quiet strength matters.

The Leaves — Clearing the Clutter

When coconut leaves dry, they become natural brooms — simple and effective. In the same way, many experienced professionals later become mentors, consultants, or guides. They help clear inefficiencies and restore order. Even if they are not at the centre anymore, their wisdom keeps the system clean and balanced.

The Shell — Fuel for Someone Else's Fire

After the fruit is used, the hard shell often becomes fuel. It burns steadily and provides warmth. Similarly, when seasoned professionals retire, their stories and lessons continue to inspire. Their contribution may no longer be active, but it still lights the way for others.

That is why I admire the coconut tree. It does not peak at one stage. Every phase has dignity. Nothing is wasted.

If we lived even partly like a coconut tree, imagine the grace with which we would move through life. Instead of constantly comparing ourselves to someone richer, younger, or more visible, we would focus on being useful in the phase we are in. Instead of chasing applause, we would chase contribution.

Because the real question is not, "How high did you rise?"

It is, "How useful were you while rising?"

That is the quiet lesson the coconut tree whispers every time the wind moves through its leaves.

The Core Idea

Tomorrow, strengthen one part of your "coconut tree." Learn a new skill, mentor someone younger, or share a lesson from your experience. Choose usefulness over comparison — and let your life grow steadily and meaningfully.

12

Seedism: The Wisdom Hidden Underground

If you observe a tree closely, you'll realise it is one of nature's most honest teachers. Everything about it is a quiet metaphor for how life truly works. You sow a seed, water it, and over time it turns into roots. Those roots grip the soil and draw nourishment, helping the tree rise. Slowly the trunk strengthens, branches spread, leaves appear, and eventually fruit arrives — colourful, sweet, admired.

And yet, when you look deeper, the roots seem to get the least recognition.

Leaves fall with the seasons. Branches may break in storms but often find new life as firewood or art. Even when the tree grows old and stops bearing fruit, the trunk is still valued — carved into furniture, polished into something that remains in homes for years.

But the roots? They disappear quietly. They did the hardest work. They held the weight. They fed the tree silently.

And when their role is complete, no one remembers them. They are not visible, not decorative, not marketable. They simply return to the soil.

The fruits, on the other hand, receive all the attention. They are photographed, admired, tasted, gifted. They are the "success stories," the glamorous results of everyone else's labour. And then — within minutes — they are consumed and forgotten.

One day it struck me: life works the same way. In families. In organisations. In society.

Some people are roots — working quietly, anchoring everything, unnoticed once the fruit appears. Some are branches — visible and supportive. Some are leaves — attractive but seasonal, moving wherever the wind takes them. And some are fruits — the ones who shine, receive praise, and enjoy the spotlight, even if only for a while.

So what should one aspire to be?

For years, I believed being the fruit was success — promotions, awards, recognition, applause. But the more I observed life, the more I realised how temporary that is. Fruits are celebrated briefly and then disappear. Leaves are seasonal. Branches weaken. Even trunks, after decades of service, are cut down once they stop producing.

Only the seed continues the journey.

The seed does something remarkable. After giving birth to the tree, it allows itself to be buried inside the fruit without ego. And when the fruit falls and fades away, the seed begins again — quietly creating the next generation. It is the only part willing to disappear and be reborn. The only part that carries forward the possibility of a forest.

That is when the idea of "Seedism" came to me — the wisdom of choosing to be the seed.

Being the seed means being comfortable without attention. It means doing your work quietly, even when praise goes elsewhere. It means understanding that real impact often happens underground — in values, habits, relationships, and unseen moments where character is shaped.

And in a strange way, the seed may be the most fulfilled part of the cycle. It does not complain that the fruit receives applause. It does not demand to be displayed like the trunk. It does not flutter for attention like the leaves. It simply creates life — again and again.

But seeds carry risks too. If ego enters the roots — "Everything exists because of me!" — the very foundation can choke the tree. When a seed becomes arrogant about being the origin, it loses its purpose. The moment humility fades, usefulness fades with it.

I have seen this in real life. Those who believed they were indispensable often found themselves replaced. Meanwhile, those who worked quietly — like seeds beneath the surface — shaped teams, families, and organisations without chasing credit.

In your career, you will meet all kinds — leaves who drift from place to place, branches who support, trunks who carry the load, fruits who shine briefly. But the rarest are the seeds — the ones who mentor quietly, build culture, shape values, and then step aside so others can grow.

Even in Indian kitchens, we preserve a small portion of curd to ferment the next batch. A simple act, yet powerful. The culture survives in that small spoonful. That is seed energy.

When you reflect on your own life, you will realise your greatest influences were seeds too — teachers who shaped you without seeking gratitude, parents who anchored your world quietly, mentors who guided you without publicity, friends who stood by you in silence. They never demanded recognition, yet without them, nothing would have grown.

Seedism, then, is simple: choose depth over display, substance over show, impact over applause.

Tomorrow, the world will celebrate its fruits again. Social media will reward what is shiny and loud. Offices will applaud the most visible performer. Society will always be drawn to what glitters.

But those who understand life know something deeper.

Growth is underground.

Growth is silent.

Growth is the seed.

The Core Idea

Tomorrow, be a seed for someone. Mentor a colleague quietly. Teach a child one small value. Help someone grow without announcing it. True legacy is created in silence — and only seeds truly understand that.

13

Unheard Today, Unforgettable Tomorrow

It's funny how life works. You say something in a meeting, and it disappears into thin air. Ten minutes later, someone with a fancier title or a louder voice repeats the same idea — and suddenly it's "brilliant," "insightful," even "visionary." You sit there thinking, *Yeh maine hi toh bola tha...*

It hurts. Being ignored chips away at confidence. Over the years, I've realised that being unheard has less to do with the quality of what we say and more to do with how people listen.

Sometimes it's simple overlooking. People are busy, distracted, or mentally prioritising what feels urgent. Attention has become expensive real estate — everyone invests it where they expect the highest return. Familiar voices often get pushed into "background noise," not because they lack value, but because routine creates blindness.

Then there's timing. A wise thought shared when no one is ready to receive it often goes unnoticed. We've all heard the story of Joshua Bell — one of the world's finest violinists — playing his priceless violin in a metro station while most people walked past. Same music. Same genius. Wrong setting. Sometimes our ideas meet the same fate.

There's another layer: the mindset of "I am OK, you are not OK." Some leaders or peers operate from a place where only their voice carries authority. Ideas coming from someone junior, quieter, or less visible are automatically seen as less credible. It isn't fair, but it happens more often than we admit.

And then there's articulation. Some people shine because they package their thoughts beautifully — the right pauses, the right stories, the right slide deck. All that glitters does get heard, at least for a while. I've attended talks that felt mesmerising in the moment, only to realise later I retained almost nothing useful. Style can temporarily overshadow substance.

Personal bias also plays its part. We all carry invisible filters. If we dislike someone, their wisdom feels lighter. It's the old saying: show me the person, and I'll show you the rule. The same sentence sounds different depending on who speaks it.

But here's what I've learned: being unheard today doesn't mean you'll be unheard forever.

Many of the thinkers and leaders we admire spent years speaking into what felt like silence. Yet they kept refining, kept showing up, kept building substance instead of chasing noise. And eventually, the world listened.

If your ideas are sincere, your intentions honest, and your work thoughtful, recognition may not arrive immediately —

but it comes steadily. Respect grows slowly, but once it takes root, it lasts.

So the next time your words seem invisible, don't lose heart. Keep showing up — with clarity, calm, and conviction. Your time will come. *Apna time aayega* is not just a catchy line; it's a quiet truth for anyone who continues doing the work.

The Core Idea

Tomorrow, instead of worrying about who is listening, focus on expressing one thought clearly and calmly — whether in a meeting, a conversation, or at home. Don't oversell it. Don't force it. Just say it well. Being heard begins with speaking without desperation. Over time, the world tunes in.

PART 3

Gratitude, Roots & the People Who Shape Us

14

The Unsung Ones Who Hold Us Up

There is a moment in the *Mahabharata* that has stayed with me for years. During the Kurukshetra war, at Krishna's request, Hanuman placed himself on Arjuna's chariot flag. From the outside, it looked symbolic — a divine emblem fluttering proudly in the wind. But something far deeper was unfolding.

Whenever Arjuna's arrows struck Karna's chariot, it rolled back by several yards. Yet when Karna's arrows hit Arjuna's chariot, it barely moved. Still, Krishna would praise Karna's strength. Arjuna couldn't understand why.

Only after the war did the truth emerge. Krishna asked Arjuna to step down first. Then he stepped down himself. And finally, when Hanuman descended from the flag, the mighty chariot — the same one that had survived countless weapons and celestial astras — collapsed and burst into flames. The only reason it had remained standing was because

Hanuman had been silently absorbing the force of the attacks. Without him, the chariot would not have lasted.

We rarely dwell on this part of the epic. Yet to me, it carries one of life's most powerful truths: the people who protect us are often invisible. They don't stand in the spotlight. They don't ask for recognition. They quietly take the blows meant for us and allow us to move forward.

If you pause and look at your own life, you'll realise you have your own Hanumans too — family members who stand behind you, friends who absorb your emotional storms, teachers who shield you from mistakes you don't even see coming, elders who take the heat so you can walk through without scars, even strangers who appear at the right time and protect you without expecting anything in return.

Think of a parent waking up early so their children can rest peacefully. A spouse who smooths life's rough edges so the other can focus on growth. A friend who defends you when you are not in the room. A sibling who takes the blame for something you did, just to keep you safe. These unseen acts are the true armour we wear — armour we rarely acknowledge.

Sometimes our unsung heroes are not even people, but moments. A chance encounter that restores confidence. A line in a book that steadies you on a difficult day. A quiet prayer said for you without your knowledge. Life is filled with invisible hands that guide, cushion, and protect.

The lesson from the *Mahabharata* is simple yet profound: never forget the ones who support you silently. They may not seek gratitude, but their absence is felt immediately. Without them, the journey becomes heavier and lonelier.

Gratitude does not require speeches. Even a small acknowledgement strengthens the bond. Sometimes, simply recognising someone's invisible contribution is enough to keep them going.

We all want to be Arjuna. But life eventually teaches us that our victories often rest on someone else's silent strength.

The Core Idea

Tomorrow, reach out to one person who has quietly supported you — a parent, sibling, colleague, friend, neighbour — and acknowledge them. No speeches. No drama. Just a simple message, a call, or a gentle word of thanks. Not because they expect it, but because you may not have reached here without them.

15

The Ones Who Wait

There's a story from the *Ramayana* that has stayed with me for years. Every time I think about it, something inside me softens. It reminds me of trust, patience, gratitude, and simple humanity.

When Lord Ram began his exile, the people of Ayodhya followed him in grief. Men, women, young, old — everyone walked behind their beloved prince, unwilling to let him go. Seeing their devotion, Ram asked them to return home, promising that he would come back after completing his fourteen-year vanvaas. Slowly, the crowd dispersed.

But not everyone left. A small group stayed back.

After completing his exile, when Ram finally returned to Ayodhya, he passed by the banks of the Tamsa river. There, he saw a group of kinnars — still waiting for him. Fourteen years had passed. Seasons had changed. Lives had moved forward. Yet they were still there. Still waiting. Still praying.

Moved, Ram asked them, "Why didn't you return when I asked everyone to go back?"

Their answer was simple, yet profound:

"You asked nar and nari to return — men and women. We are neither. So we stayed."

That one line carries immense devotion and identity. They did not follow logic, convenience, or advantage. They followed their hearts.

Ram was deeply touched and blessed them with the power to give *badhai* — blessings believed to carry special grace. Even today, long after kingdoms have changed, that cultural memory continues.

This story leaves me with many reflections.

Some people obey out of fear. Some obey for benefit. But some follow because love leaves them no other choice. Devotion born from love — not fear — has a different strength.

I also think about the waiting. We live in times where patience is rare. We expect instant replies, quick promotions, immediate results. Yet here were people who waited fourteen years — with no updates, no guarantees, no visibility into the future. Only faith.

And when Ram returned, he did not overlook them. He acknowledged them. He honoured them.

If even God paused to recognise those who stood by him, should we not do the same?

This story also reminds me of the dignity the kinnar community deserves. Their place in our society is rooted in history and faith. At the very least, we can offer respect, inclusion, and humanity.

Ultimately, stories like this remind me that walking the path of Ram — a life of dignity, restraint, empathy, and righteousness — is not easy, but always worth striving for. The world will test you. But if you can respond with grace when tired and compassion when stressed, you are walking toward dharma.

The Core Idea

Tomorrow, express gratitude to someone who has quietly supported you — a driver, a colleague, a parent, a helper at home, anyone. Send a message. Make a call. Say a genuine "thank you." It may take you ten seconds. But for someone who has been silently waiting to be seen, it may mean everything.

16

The Three People We Carry Within

My daughter was travelling in Taiwan when she came across a sculpture that stopped her in her tracks. She sent me a picture along with the artist's words, and I must have read them ten times.

"There is a you, a me, and another person entwined in people's hearts, with the three sharing the same pair of legs. Who would be the one to instruct the legs to walk in unison? This work presents a state of inner turmoil, reflecting the many different facets of the human heart. As the external world gradually presses closer to a person, this entangled and unsettled phenomenon of the heart becomes even more apparent."

It struck me immediately. The sculpture was more than art; it was a mirror of modern life — of our inner chaos, of the constant push and pull we carry within us.

The older I grow, the clearer it becomes: life is often about learning to walk with three sets of desires, duties, and impulses tugging at the same pair of legs. Some days they move in harmony. On others, they pull in different directions, leaving us confused and emotionally tangled.

But everyone goes through this — you, me, and the artist who created that sculpture. We simply don't say it aloud.

When I reflected on it, five interpretations came to mind — five versions of ourselves we balance every day.

First: yourself, your spouse, your children.

Every home carries this invisible three-way pull. You want peace. Your spouse wants order. Your child wants freedom. One leg moves towards discipline. Another towards affection. The third towards understanding. In the middle of it all, you are simply trying to stay balanced.

I've seen parents come home exhausted, while a partner wants to discuss responsibilities and a child wants attention — all at the same moment. Whose need do you prioritise? Who teaches the "legs" to move together? These are not problems you solve; they are realities you learn to manage.

Second: health, wealth, and family.

We sacrifice health to earn wealth. Then we use wealth to recover health. Meanwhile, family quietly absorbs the cost. Some chase financial stability and miss important moments at home. Others prioritise family and worry about career growth. Again three pulls, one pair of legs.

Third: yourself, your superior, your subordinates.

Anyone in a workplace understands this tension. The boss wants speed. The team wants clarity. You want balance. Walking in all three directions at once is not easy. Sometimes one side feels disappointed. Sometimes all three do.

Fourth: yourself, your country, your religion.

We want modern lives, yet our roots shape us deeply. We think globally, yet local identities influence us. We seek personal freedom while valuing collective harmony. One leg steps toward progress, another toward tradition, and the third toward belonging. It is not about right or wrong — it is about balance.

And finally — the most personal tug-of-war: mind, body, and soul.

The mind wants excitement. The body wants rest. The soul wants peace.

When we ignore one, restlessness grows. That unsettled feeling the artist described becomes familiar.

So how do we walk without falling when these forces constantly pull at us?

In my experience, five qualities help steady the steps.

Resilience — because alignment does not happen every day.

Adjustment — because harmony requires compromise.

Adaptability — because life keeps changing.

Empathy — because the other "figures" in your life have struggles too.

Big-picture thinking — because long-term clarity reduces short-term conflict.

When these are anchored by a strong inner compass — your conscience — you stop trying to untangle every knot. You learn to walk even when everything is not perfectly aligned. You understand that life is less about choosing one heart over another and more about finding a rhythm where they coexist.

And gradually, the chaos softens.

That is the beauty of the sculpture. It offers no solution — only recognition.

A quiet reminder that feeling pulled in different directions does not mean you are weak. It means you are human.

The Core Idea

Tomorrow, switch off your phone for ten minutes. Let it be a small untangling — a pause where your mind, emotions, and duties stop pulling at you. Those ten minutes will not solve everything, but they may remind you that balance begins with a single moment of calm.

17

The Little Eyes Watching Us

I recently landed at Delhi airport and did what every traveller does on stepping out — I called home. My son-in-law picked up immediately. "Papa, thoda jam hai near Terminal 3. Bas aa raha hoon." His tone was so casual that I assumed I'd be in the car within fifteen minutes.

But destiny — and Delhi traffic — had other plans.

That "thoda" jam stretched into three long hours. Three hours to cover barely two kilometres. By the time he reached the arrival gate, the poor fellow looked like he had fought a mini-Kurukshetra of honking, bumper-to-bumper crawling, and repeated "Sir, aage badho" exchanges with cab drivers. My twin grandsons in the backseat were a delightful mix of chaos and charm — excited to see me, restless from the delay, puzzled about why "Dadu ka ghar is so far," and tired of being strapped in for so long.

It was the kind of episode adults want to forget the moment they reach home.

But children don't forget so easily.

Their minds store impressions the way soft clay holds fingerprints — clearly and permanently.

A few days later, my phone pinged with a picture from my son-in-law. It showed one of my grandsons sitting cross-legged on the living room floor, arranging his toy cars into a perfect, winding line. At the end of this "traffic queue," he had placed his toy aeroplane, facing the cars. The caption read:

"We are going to the airport. Stuck in traffic jam."

That single image said more about *sanskaras* than any scripture could. A three-hour ordeal that the adults wanted to erase had already settled into a child's imagination, becoming part of his inner world.

This is how sanskaras are formed — quietly, subtly, without announcements or sermons. Children absorb everything they see. No filters. No judgement. No analysis. They simply watch. And what they watch becomes the raw material of their personality.

Growing up, our own sanskaras came from the environment around us. Most of us learned courtesy not from textbooks but from watching our parents fold their hands in namaste. We saw elders offer water before asking questions. We observed them speak gently even when tired. We learned dignity by seeing our grandparents live simply and give generously.

Indian culture has long understood that values are not "taught." They are caught.

That is why stories were such an important part of childhood. Vikram-Betaal, Panchatantra, Sant Kabir — these stories planted seeds of courage, honesty, and compassion long before we had the maturity to debate them. The impressions stayed.

Today, much has changed. Children absorb more from screens than from people. Their ears often hear more stress than surrender, more comparison than confidence. A society that once encouraged "Atithi Devo Bhava" now says, "Don't open the door — it may not be safe." A home that once echoed with "Pehle aap" now echoes with "Hurry up, we're late!"

The world has become more complex, and caution is understandable. But one principle remains unchanged: children absorb what they see.

A child who sees shouting assumes shouting is normal.

A child who sees gratitude learns gratitude.

A child who sees kindness practises kindness.

A child who sees respect offers respect.

It is rarely the big, dramatic moments that shape a child. It is the small, daily actions.

A mother giving her seat to an elderly person.

A father returning extra change to the sabziwala.

A parent saying sorry after losing their temper.

A family eating together without devices.

A grandparent praying quietly each morning.

These become templates for a child's moral compass.

Children don't need lectures. They need examples. They are watching when we discuss relatives, when we drive, when we tip, when we speak to waiters, when we honour commitments, when we handle frustration.

Sanskaras are not created in temples alone. They are formed in living rooms, at dining tables, in grocery stores, during car rides — and yes, even in traffic jams that last three hours.

Every day, we are imprinting something.

The only question is: are we imprinting what we want them to carry for life?

That little line of toy cars reminded me that even ordinary moments become a child's lifelong emotional album.

The Core Idea

Tomorrow, consciously model one small behaviour you want your child or grandchild to absorb — your tone while speaking, the way you handle frustration, how you greet someone, or how you express gratitude. Beautiful sanskaras grow from tiny, everyday seeds.

18

The Shoulders We Stand On

A few mornings ago, I stepped out onto my balcony with my usual cup of tea. The sunlight was sharp, almost theatrical, and right in the middle of it stood a red rose — glowing as if the sun had chosen it for a spotlight.

Right beside it was another rose, wilted and leaning, the kind no one pauses to admire anymore. The contrast was striking. One flower was basking in attention; the other swayed gently in the wind, as if to say, "I mattered too, once."

And suddenly, it struck me — this is how workplace cycles unfold.

When someone new rises, full of energy and ideas, attention shifts instantly. The older colleague, the one who once held the ship steady, slowly fades into the background. The world loves newness.

But in our rush to admire the fresh bloom, we forget the flower that helped the plant stand tall in the first place.

Why does this happen?

I've seen it often.

A young professional gets promoted, grows confident, gains visibility — and slowly begins to look at their mentor with impatience.

"Maybe I don't need him anymore."

"Maybe she's slowing me down."

"Maybe I've outgrown them."

It's rarely deliberate. Growth makes us look forward. Ego makes us forget to look back.

But that morning, the rose reminded me of something important:

Ignoring the one who shaped you does not diminish them. It diminishes you.

Mentors are not obstacles. They are accelerators.

Over the years, I've noticed something consistent — the most successful people never "outgrow" their mentors. They deepen their gratitude. Because when everything goes well, the world applauds you. But when something cracks — a failed project, a broken relationship, shaken confidence — it is often your mentor who stands quietly behind you, ready to steady you.

Mentors do not seek praise or position. They care.

Here is what mentors truly offer:

• Course correction

Experience is another way of saying, "I've seen this mistake before." A mentor can sense the road ahead without needing Google Maps.

• A guardian, not a competitor

Youth sometimes forgets this: your mentor is the only person in the room who wants you to grow without wanting your chair.

- **Unfiltered truth**

Friends may comfort you. Colleagues may be diplomatic. A mentor tells you what you need to hear.

- **Roots that allow branches to grow**

The fruit may shine, but the seed did the unseen work. Nothing flourishes without what came before.

- **A shoulder on difficult days**

Not many in your professional circle will offer that.

There's a simple habit in our homes that reflects this beautifully. We save a spoonful of old curd to set the next batch. That tiny starter transforms the entire bowl. Mentors are like that — quiet "starter cultures" that ferment strength into your future.

The Core Idea

Tomorrow, think of one mentor — a teacher, a senior colleague, an elder — someone who quietly shaped who you are. Send a message. Make a call. Say a simple thank you. Gratitude keeps you grounded. And roots are what help you grow.

PART 4

Inner Peace, Faith & Emotional Courage

19

Where Peace Begins: A Personal Note on Letting Go

Sometimes, when I sit quietly in the evenings, I find myself thinking about people I haven't spoken to in a while. No major reason — just small hurts and misunderstandings that slowly piled up. A careless remark. A message left on "seen." A tone that didn't sit right. And without noticing, a tiny crack becomes a wall.

On such evenings, I softly recite the Jain forgiveness mantra:

Khamemi Savve Jiva — I forgive everyone.

Savve Jiva Khamantu me — May everyone forgive me.

Each time, it feels as though someone has gently placed a hand on my shoulder and said, "You don't have to carry all this." Because the truth is, most of us are carrying more than we admit.

Sometimes it's an old friendship we didn't know how to repair.

Sometimes it's a family moment we wish had unfolded differently.

Sometimes it's our own mistake — the one we haven't forgiven ourselves for.

One conversation changed how I saw forgiveness.

A colleague once told me she hadn't spoken to her elder sister in three years.

"Why?" I asked.

She shrugged. "I don't even remember the exact reason anymore. But neither of us wants to message first."

Three years.

Over something neither could clearly explain.

It struck me because it is so common. Silence becomes heavy, yet pride keeps it in place. That evening, I thought about people I had drifted from — some because of me, some because of them, most because life simply moved on. But I was still carrying the unfinished story inside.

That is when the prayer began to make deeper sense.

It is not just a mantra. It is a reminder:

Mitti me Savva Bhooesu — Let friendship exist.

Veram Majjham Na Kenai — Let no bitterness remain.

Bitterness seems small, but it grows quietly — like weeds in an untended garden.

Real forgiveness is not dramatic. It does not require speeches or background music. Often, forgiveness looks like:

Deleting an angry draft message.

Unclenching your jaw when someone's name comes up.

Admitting, "Yes, I'm hurt — but I don't want to stay hurt."

Letting a memory pass without replaying the argument.

Accepting that you deserve peace — even if an apology never arrives.

It is small.

It is private.

It is for you.

Life gives us daily opportunities to practise this.

When a colleague takes credit for your idea.

When your child snaps at you after a long day.

When someone cuts ahead in line.

When a friend forgets to call back.

When a family member speaks carelessly.

When a stranger honks impatiently on the road.

None of these are life-changing events. But if we keep collecting them, they quietly shape our inner world.

Forgiveness works like a reset button. An emotional detox. Just as we declutter wardrobes and kitchen shelves, imagine decluttering your mind — one hurt at a time.

The world often tells us to hold our ground, win arguments, prove points.

But sometimes the strongest choice is simpler:

I choose peace.

I choose softness.

I choose to let go.

And that choice changes you.

The Core Idea

Tomorrow, release one small grudge — the tiniest one you are holding. A forgotten apology. A rude comment. An old irritation. Put it down. Forgiveness is not something you give others. It is freedom you give yourself.

20

Inner Intelligence (II): Seeing What We Already Have

We often look at life through the lens of what's missing — the job we didn't get, the money we wish we had, the comfort someone else seems to enjoy. Sometimes, it takes a very simple moment to remind us of the wealth we already carry.

A friend once told me about something he witnessed at a traffic signal. A young beggar approached a man sitting in his car and said softly, "Sir, kuch de do… something to eat."

The man asked him, "Why don't you work?"

The boy shrugged. "God has not been kind to me."

Instead of arguing, the man paused and asked calmly, "Tell me something… would you sell one of your eyes for five lakhs?"

The boy looked stunned. "No! How can I give my eye?"

"Alright," the man continued, "what about a kidney? For twenty-five lakhs?"

Now the boy was annoyed. "Why are you saying such things?"

The man slowly stepped out of the car. He walked with a limp, supported by a crutch.

He said gently, "You think God hasn't been kind to you? Look at me. I lost a leg in an accident. My left eye barely sees. My kidneys need constant monitoring. I would give everything I have to get back what you take for granted."

The boy fell silent. Something shifted in him. He walked away — not angrily, but thoughtfully.

My friend said that moment stayed with him for days. It stayed with me too.

Because it reminded me of something we forget almost every morning:

If you opened your eyes today…

If you walked to the bathroom on your own…

If you stretched your arms without assistance…

You are already wealthier than you think.

We don't need constant motivation. We need awareness.

Spend one minute tomorrow morning looking at yourself in the mirror and acknowledging the gift of a functioning body. It sounds simple, but it grounds you instantly.

And then — close your eyes.

The darkness you see is not only from your eyelids. It is also from the layers we build inside:

- resentment
- jealousy
- greed
- small dishonesties we justify
- grudges we polish and protect

These do not just cloud the mind — they dim our inner intelligence.

Inner Intelligence, or II, is not about IQ, degrees, or titles. It is the quiet voice that tells you when something feels right or wrong. It is the steady flame within that burns brighter when you act with integrity — and flickers when you don't.

If you remove even one layer each day — a little less envy, a little more kindness, a little more honesty — you will notice something surprising. You begin to sense light even with your eyes closed. That is clarity. That is II — the truest form of intelligence.

Today, of course, we all use AI — Artificial Intelligence. It is powerful. It helps us think faster, write better, and work smarter.

But the decisions that shape our lives — whom we love, what we stand for, how we act when no one is watching — come only from II, not AI.

Use AI to improve efficiency.

Use II to improve your life.

The Core Idea

Tomorrow morning, do two simple things: Look into the mirror and say thank you for the body you have. Then close your eyes and ask yourself: What darkness am I ready to release today? Clear even a little of it — and you may find your inner light waiting quietly on the other side.

21

GOD Chat

We live in a world where, with the right prompt, strong connectivity, and a reliable platform, you can ask almost anything and receive an answer instantly. A recipe, a philosophical doubt, a work problem — ChatGPT has quietly become everyone's go-to "friend."

One day, half joking and half curious, I wondered: If we can connect with AI so easily, why can't we connect with God in the same way? After all, prayer is also a kind of chat window — just without a keyboard.

So one quiet morning, I closed my eyes and imagined typing on the screen of my mind:

"God Chat — Connecting…"

To my surprise, I felt an answer — not in sound, but clear enough to understand:

"Yes, my child. Ask."

And just like that, the conversation began.

"God, why is there so much suffering in the world?"

The response felt calm and familiar:

"Because I gave every human the freedom to act. I do not control their choices — only the fruits of those choices. Action is yours. Result is mine. That balance is my Constitution."

It reminded me instantly of the Gita: *Karmanye vadhikaraste…* We are responsible for action, not ownership of outcomes. Every joy and sorrow flows through karma.

"Do You listen to everyone's prayers?"

The reply was simple:

"I listen to all prayers.

But I respond quickly to those born from compassion, service, and kindness.

Prayers rooted in greed or ego?

I let them fade on their own."

That struck me. Perhaps God is not ignoring us. Perhaps He is filtering.

"Why did You create so many religions? So many castes? So many differences?"

I could almost sense a smile in the reply:

"I created seasons, and no one complained. I made different fruits, trees, rivers, and colours — and you enjoy them all. Why should diversity among people be any different? Each religion is a flower. Together they form a garland. Separate them, and each one loses its fragrance."

Such a simple perspective. We complicate what the universe designed effortlessly.

The conversation continued, and I lost track of time.

Finally, I asked what many of us quietly wonder:

"God, how do I stay connected to You?"

The answer felt gentle, almost like it rose from within: "Align the strings of your mind with mine. No password. No subscription. No data charges. This connection runs on two things — love and faith. That is the platform. That is 'God Chat.'"

The Core Idea

Tomorrow morning, before reaching for your phone, sit quietly for two minutes. Ask whatever is on your mind. Don't wait for a thunderbolt or a voice from the sky. Just ask with sincerity — and listen with faith. Because the oldest chat platform in the world isn't WhatsApp, Gmail, or ChatGPT. It is the one powered by silence, connection, and trust. And it is always online.

22

Stay True to Yourself

The more I observe the world around me, the more I realise that modern peer pressure has very little to do with teenagers anymore. It follows us into adulthood — into workplaces, homes, and even holidays.

A few weeks ago, a friend told me about her daughter who returned from school upset. When someone asked where she had gone for her summer vacation, she said proudly, "Thailand." It was her first international trip with her parents. They had saved for months, planned carefully, and created beautiful memories.

But before she could finish, a few children interrupted:

"Bas Thailand? We went to eleven countries!"

"We stayed on a private island!"

"We took a cruise!"

Her excitement disappeared in seconds. She came home saying she felt "small."

That stayed with me. Not because the other children travelled more — that's fine — but because we adults have quietly built a world where "more" has become the new definition of "better."

More holidays.

More countries.

More cars.

More money.

More likes.

More everything.

And if you don't keep pace, you start feeling inadequate.

Peer pressure today is subtle. It hides in casual conversations, Instagram posts, cars parked outside homes, the size of dinner bills, the brand of your phone. Earlier, it lived in school corridors. Now it walks into boardrooms and family WhatsApp groups.

I see families with three cars for four people — not because they need them, but because "everyone has multiple cars now." Then we sit in traffic jams, breathing polluted air, wondering why our cities are choking.

And don't get me started on phones.

Every time a new model launches, perfectly good phones suddenly feel outdated. Overnight, the device that worked beautifully yesterday now feels embarrassing.

I know someone who buys a new phone every year. Not because the old one is broken. No. The old one lies at home with 128 GB of unused memory, wondering what mistake it made.

I once asked him, "Why upgrade every year? What did this phone do to you?"

He replied, "Arre yaar, this one has a new camera mode."

I told him, "It's fine if you want the new phone. Just don't blame the old one. It still calls, takes photos, sends

WhatsApps, sets alarms, even reminds you to drink water. What more do you want — should it cook dinner too?"

He laughed because he knew the truth.

The phone wasn't the issue. Peer pressure was.

We upgrade because:

"Everyone in the team did."

"My cousin has this model."

"This notch is smaller."

"It comes in a new colour."

And the funniest part? The moment you buy it, the next version is announced. Your brand-new phone becomes old within weeks.

If that isn't proof that chasing trends is endless, what is?

When did contentment become outdated?

When did simplicity become embarrassing?

When did "enough" stop being enough?

Staying true to yourself today requires quiet courage. It means choosing a holiday you can comfortably afford — not one that empties your savings for a social media caption. It means buying a car because you need it — not because your neighbour bought two. It means living at a pace that suits your mind, not the world's noise.

I once had a colleague who refused to buy a smartphone until he truly needed one. For years, people teased him. He would smile and say, "When I need it, I'll buy it." And when he finally did, many around him — overwhelmed by constant notifications — envied the peaceful years he had enjoyed.

Peer pressure is strange. It makes you chase things you never truly wanted. Slowly, without noticing, you drift away from yourself.

I remind myself often:

There will always be someone richer.

Someone more travelled.

Someone with a flashier lifestyle.

But there is only one you — with your needs, your dreams, your priorities, your truth.

If you stay honest with yourself, you will never feel behind.

The Core Idea

Tomorrow, don't try to match the world. Do one thing your way — choose, buy, say, or decide something simply because you want it, not because others expect it. That is what staying true to yourself looks like. Not dramatic declarations. Just small, steady choices that feel peaceful inside. Because happiness is not measured in countries visited, cars owned, or photos posted. It is measured in how comfortably you can live in your own skin — without needing the world's approval.

23

The Gift of a Well-Placed "No"

We all know Dhritarashtra from the Mahabharata — an overly attached father who was blind not only in sight, but in judgment. He indulged his sons, especially Duryodhana, because he could not bear the discomfort of saying no. And we know how that story ended: a kingdom lost, a family destroyed.

Most modern parents don't realise it, but we often stand where Dhritarashtra once stood. We confuse love with approval, affection with indulgence, and validation with care.

It's uncomfortable to admit, but true: a child who never hears "no" grows up believing they are entitled to "yes" everywhere.

And life doesn't work that way.

I remember visiting a friend's home and witnessing a small disagreement between him and his young daughter. We were all new to parenting then, still learning. She wanted a fancier school bag because her classmates had switched to trendier ones. It was an ordinary request — one most parents would fulfil without hesitation.

But my friend stood firm. "Your bag is not broken or torn," he said calmly.

The girl protested, shed a few tears, and went to her room.

Later, I asked him if he had been too harsh. He replied, "I don't want her school life to become a race for validation — wearing what others wear, buying what others buy, carrying what 'fits in.' And I still remember what the Principal told us on the first day: parents must learn to say the occasional 'no.'"

That small moment stayed with me. While always trying to be gentle with my daughters, I also tried to keep them grounded. It wasn't perfect. There were hiccups. But I like to believe they grew up strong and self-confident, not easily shaken by comparison.

Today, we see children demanding toys in supermarkets — and parents giving in to avoid a scene. Teenagers asking for the latest gadgets — and parents agreeing because "all their friends have it." Young adults struggling with the smallest setback because they've rarely faced disappointment at home.

But what happens when life finally says no?

Because it will.

A college rejection.

A failed exam.

An unreturned love.

A missed promotion.

Life does not soften its blows.

A child who grows up believing every desire must be fulfilled often becomes an adult who fractures at the first crack. I've met such people — bright, capable, talented — but emotionally fragile. One setback feels like betrayal. One criticism feels unbearable.

Perhaps because no one taught them that frustration is not a catastrophe. It is part of growth.

On the other hand, children who hear the occasional "no," spoken with love and clarity, develop resilience. They learn that worth does not depend on possessions. They understand that disappointment is survivable. They begin to build inner strength instead of seeking constant validation.

Our scriptures echo this truth.

Kaikeyi loved her son — but love mixed with entitlement led to exile and sorrow. Gandhari loved her sons — but chose blindness over correction. Affection without responsibility often ends in regret.

Even in modern life, the pattern repeats. The child who gets everything often values nothing. The teenager shielded from every hardship becomes the employee who cannot handle feedback. The son never told "enough" struggles with boundaries. The daughter never corrected may confuse indulgence with love.

As parents, our role is not to be heroes, but guides. To set direction. To create boundaries. To say no when the path is wrong — even if it invites temporary anger.

Children do not need a perfect world. They need a real one.

In the real world, people will not always applaud them. They will not always agree with them. They will certainly not give them everything they ask for.

If we do not teach them how to handle "no," the world will — and far more harshly.

The Core Idea

Sometimes we must be firm to truly be kind. Say "no" to an unreasonable demand — not out of ego, but out of love. One thoughtful, well-placed "no" can build more character than a hundred easy yeses. In the long run, your child will not remember the bag, the toy, or the gadget. But they will remember the lesson. And one day, they may even thank you for it.

PART 5

India, Wisdom & the Collective Soul

24

Ten Lessons I Brought Back from the Mahakumbh

Before visiting the Mahakumbh, I thought I understood scale, discipline, and devotion. In my professional life, we often speak of "mass outreach," "large rollouts," and "complex coordination." But nothing — truly nothing — prepared me for what I witnessed at Prayagraj.

The Mahakumbh did not feel like an event. It felt like a peaceful revolution, powered by patience, grace, and faith.

Here are the ten lessons I carried home with me.

1. Scale is discipline in motion.

Standing at the Sangam, watching lakhs of devotees move in order without pushing or shouting, I realised something profound: systems alone do not create order — people do. No manual can teach what ordinary Indians demonstrated naturally — self-regulation, courtesy, and collective responsibility.

2. Patience is India's oldest superpower.

At one point, traffic was stuck for hours. Anywhere else, tempers would have flared. Here, people waited quietly. An elderly man smiled and said, "Beta, Sangam toh wahin hai. Jaldi kyun?" That one sentence captured the calm resilience that has sustained this country for centuries.

3. Vasudhaiva Kutumbakam is not a slogan — it is lived.

I saw sons carrying fathers, daughters walking hand in hand with mothers, saints postponing their own amrit-snaan so others could go first, and strangers offering tea and prasad. It was unity in its most natural form.

4. The youth are not disconnecting.

The energy of young devotees surprised me. They were not there merely for spectacle or social media. They were sincere and deeply engaged. Many said the experience changed something within them — made them want to live more consciously.

5. Setbacks reveal real leadership.

One morning, a sudden change in arrangements caused delays and mild restlessness. Then a senior saint walked through the crowd, hands folded, and said softly, "Sabr rakho, sab ho jayega." That was all. The mood shifted instantly. I realised leadership is often not about instruction — it is about presence.

6. Good communication amplifies good intent.

From banners to digital screens, from announcements to apps, messaging reached every corner. Even centuries-old traditions require clear, modern communication to connect with a contemporary audience.

7. The economy thrives where humanity lives.

For thousands — vendors, boatmen, tent owners, drivers, artisans — the Kumbh is livelihood. No shopping mall or online sale can replicate this grassroots uplift. It is economic activity woven with dignity and faith.

8. Technology is serving tradition — not replacing it.

Drones, CCTV cameras, heatmaps, GPS tracking, real-time alerts — the entire ecosystem functioned like a global operation. Ancient rituals and modern infrastructure worked side by side in harmony.

9. Faith is the ultimate project manager.

Despite delays, crowds, and unpredictability, one belief held steady: "Snan hoga." And it did. Every time. When purpose is shared and intention is pure, coordination becomes organic. I have seen small teams argue over minor tasks. Here, millions aligned effortlessly — because they were united by faith.

10. The real revolution is inner, not outer.

When I stepped into the icy waters of the Sangam, surrounded by soft chants, I felt an inner stillness I cannot fully describe. Devotion has a certain frequency. When millions tune into it together, something shifts within you. The Mahakumbh may be the only revolution powered entirely by peace, humility, and belief.

The Core Idea

Tomorrow, take one small "mental dip." Cleanse one negative thought, one lingering resentment, or one old irritation. The Mahakumbh reminds us that purification begins not with scale — but with a single, quiet decision.

25

Where Are You Going So Fast?

The other day, I was driving along an ordinary stretch of road when a car shot past me so quickly that even the leaves seemed to flutter in its wake. I'm not exaggerating — the man was flying. I could see his triumphant grin in the rearview mirror, the kind that says, "I won. I'm ahead."

I smiled to myself. I've seen this movie before.

Five minutes later, I saw him again. Not racing. Not grinning. But stuck behind a slow-moving garbage truck, drumming his fingers on the steering wheel while life moved at its own pace.

At the next red light, we stopped side by side. For a moment, he looked genuinely puzzled — as if the universe had played a small joke on him. All that urgency, all that effort… and here we were, exactly together.

That's when the thought crossed my mind: Where exactly are we all going so fast?

Somewhere along the way, speed became a virtue. People proudly say they're "rushing," "multitasking," "swamped," "running non-stop." It has become fashionable to be exhausted. Fast emails, fast promotions, fast meals, fast opinions — we've turned urgency into identity.

Let me say this honestly: I believe in staying ahead. In being early. Prepared. Disciplined. These habits have helped me throughout life.

But staying ahead is not the same as rushing ahead.

One brings peace. The other brings pressure.

I've seen this clearly in real life. A friend of mine lived every day at triple speed — quick meals, quick decisions, quick conversations. His family adjusted for years. Vacations became checklists. Dinners became briefings. Even celebrations felt hurried.

One day, his wife told him quietly, "I want to live at my pace, not at the speed of your deadlines."

She wasn't angry anymore. She was tired.

Life has its own rhythm. Some things unfold only when they're ready — relationships, healing, wisdom, happiness. You cannot force them. If you rush them, they resist. If you push them, they break. *Sehej pake so meetha hoye.*

Nature understands this well. The sun rises at its own pace. A seed sprouts when it is ready. Spring arrives only after winter leaves.

But we behave like that driver — always overtaking, often without knowing the destination.

Rushing blinds us. We miss the taste of breakfast, the softness of the morning air, the warmth in someone's voice. We also miss warning signs — stress, fatigue, irritability. By the time we slow down, the cost has already been paid.

Once, at a grocery store, I watched an elderly man count coins slowly at the counter. The line behind him grew restless. People sighed. A few rolled their eyes. But he continued calmly, unmoved by the world's tempo.

That day I realised — he wasn't slow. We were too fast.

Every philosophy says the same thing in different words. The Gita speaks of balance — *yuktahara viharasya* — moderation in all things. Jain dharma speaks of restraint. Buddhism centres on mindful movement and mindful breath.

Every time we rush, we exchange peace for pressure.

And often, we don't even know what we're chasing. Validation? Fear of missing out? The illusion that faster means better?

The irony is that rushing rarely gets us there sooner — just like that driver at the red light. It only makes us tired.

Slowing down does not mean doing less. It means doing with presence.

When we slow down, even simple moments deepen. Tea tastes richer. A walk feels calmer. A conversation becomes meaningful. A problem becomes easier because the mind is no longer sprinting.

We assume speed equals progress. But sometimes progress hides in stillness — in pausing long enough to think clearly, listen fully, breathe deeply.

And I won't give you a long list of habits to change. Lists create more pressure.

Just one small resolution.

The Core Idea

Tomorrow, choose one thing you usually rush — and do it slowly. Just one. Not your entire day. Not every habit. Maybe your drive. Your tea. Your shower. Your walk. Or your first conversation of the morning. Do it slowly. Deliberately. With attention. Notice how the moment shifts. Notice how you shift. Because slowing down one moment has a way of softening all the others. Life is not a race to the next red light. Sometimes, the real victory lies in arriving gently — not first.

26

How India Played Its Way to Health

A few days ago, I walked past the old ground where we once spent entire evenings. The swings were still there. The dust was still soft underfoot. But something was missing — people. Not a single child. Not a single voice. Just silence.

And I remembered how, in our time, we had to be dragged home from the playground.

"Bas five minutes aur!"

Whether it was eating, studying, bathing, or sleeping — everything was delayed because someone had shouted, "Last round!" or "One more game!"

Today?

Parents struggle to push children outdoors.

Even adults prefer screens over sunlight.

And the more sedentary we become, the more we spend on gyms — as if we are trying to replace something our bodies still quietly miss.

The Games That Built Us without Us Realising

We never thought of them as workouts. They were simply fun.

Gilli Danda — reflexes and coordination

Kabaddi — stamina, strength, breath control

Kancha — focus and posture

Pitthu — agility and teamwork

Kite flying — balance and patience

Kho-Kho — speed and strategy

Stapu (Hopscotch) — balance and core strength

Chess and Carrom — focus and mental discipline

All this, free of cost. No memberships. No special shoes. No trackers. No protein shakes.

And it wasn't just games.

Life itself was exercise.

Our grandparents didn't "work out." They simply lived — and that was enough.

Grinding wheat on the chakki was upper-body training.

Walking long distances was natural cardio.

Climbing trees built flexibility and courage.

Washing clothes by hand strengthened arms.

Squatting kept joints supple.

Cleaning courtyards improved mobility.

Sitting cross-legged strengthened the core.

No one counted steps. Movement was woven into the day.

Fitness was never the goal.

It was the by-product of living fully.

What Changed?

Slowly, we moved from:

natural → artificial
playful → structured
simple → complicated
free movement → paid exercise
Outdoor evenings became indoor scrolling.
Unplanned joy became scheduled workouts.
Effortless fitness became effortful fitness.

But the body remembers. It knows the difference between living and merely burning calories.

The Core Idea

Tomorrow, revive one childhood movement — just one. Not a gym routine. Not a challenge you'll abandon in a week. Just one simple act your younger self enjoyed: Play a quick game of hopscotch. Fly a kite from the terrace. Walk barefoot on grass. Sweep your balcony yourself. Sit on the floor and stand up ten times. Throw a ball against a wall. Dust off your carrom board. One tiny movement that reconnects you with the joy your body once knew. Not to lose weight. Not to build muscle. But to remember how it feels to be fully alive.

27

Build a Business on Worth, Not a Gamble

I've always believed a business should feel like a temple built brick by brick — steady, honest, meaningful. You place one brick carefully, make sure it holds, then add another. Slowly, a structure rises. It may not be flashy, but it is strong. It stands because it has been built on worth.

Now compare that with a castle of cards. Attractive. Exciting. But one small gust of air and everything collapses. That, to me, is what business becomes when it is built on speculation, shortcuts, and the urge to "hit it big" overnight.

I've seen people jump into ventures simply because "others are making money there," or because a trend is going viral, or because some video promised overnight crores. It is gambling dressed up as entrepreneurship.

The Mahabharata offers one of the greatest warnings about this mindset. The Pandavas — capable and respected — did not lose their kingdom on the battlefield. They lost it at a gambling table. Not because they lacked strength, but because they relied on chance instead of character.

Even the strongest can fall when they gamble with their foundation.

Over the years, watching businesses rise and fall, I've noticed one clear difference between those who endure and those who collapse:

Some build for value.

Some chase valuation.

You can often predict who will last.

I once met a young man running a small service business. Nothing extravagant — just decent, honest work. One day he said, "Sir, others in my industry have doubled their prices. I think I should too."

I asked him, "Has your service doubled in quality?"

He fell silent.

That's the problem with shortcuts. A simple question exposes them.

On the other hand, I knew a woman who started a small tiffin service from home. She woke at 4 a.m., cooked with care, and personally checked every dabba before it went out. Her prices were fair. Her service was consistent. Today she runs a full kitchen with a team and a waiting list. She built worth first. Income followed.

This is something I believe deeply:

When money becomes the goal, the business becomes fragile.

When purpose becomes the goal, money becomes the by-product.

Money is restless. It comes and goes. But usefulness lasts.

If your work solves a real problem, if it improves someone's day, if customers feel respected, you have already built a durable business model.

Look at the biggest brands in the world. None began with, "Let's make a lot of money." They began with:

"How do we connect people?"

"How do we organise information?"

"How do we make life easier?"

Purpose first. Profit next.

You can see the same principle in small roadside businesses. The chaiwala who remembers exactly how strong his regular customer likes his tea builds loyalty faster than the one counting cash all day. The tailor who listens carefully earns trust that no discount can buy.

When you build on worth, you build reputation. And reputation does not fluctuate like markets.

Businesses built on speculation rarely allow peaceful sleep. You are constantly waiting — for markets to rise, for trends to hold, for luck to continue. It feels like standing on quicksand.

But when you build something genuinely useful — even slowly — you sleep better. You know what you offer. You know why you exist. And when storms arrive, customers stay.

There is another danger in chasing shortcuts — the pressure to imitate. One viral "millionaire idea," and thousands rush to copy it without asking:

Does this align with my skills?

Do I believe in it?

Does the world truly need it?

In the rush to strike gold, we forget that real gold is forged patiently — through fire, endurance, and intention.

Years later, when someone finally succeeds honestly, people call them lucky. They see the temple. They forget the bricks.

A business is a living entity. It absorbs your values. If you start with greed, it weakens. If you start with service, it strengthens.

Maybe slower.

Maybe quieter.

But infinitely more stable.

The Core Idea

Tomorrow, take ten quiet minutes and ask yourself: "If money were removed from the equation, what would I still want my work or business to stand for?" Write down the answer. That is your foundation. Build from there — a temple, not a house of cards.

28

Trust the Process

One of the simplest yet most powerful lines from the Bhagavad Gita is this: *"You have the right to your actions, but not to the results."*

It sounds beautiful. But try living it — that's when the real test begins.

There are moments when life feels unfair. We work hard for weeks or months, only to watch someone else receive the credit. We prepare diligently for an exam or interview, yet our name doesn't appear on the list.

"Why work so hard if results aren't guaranteed?" I have asked myself that question many times.

The answer did not arrive instantly. It took years to understand that the only part of life we truly control is the process — never the outcome.

Whenever someone says effort goes to waste, I think of those who made it against all odds simply because they persisted.

I think of *The Pursuit of Happyness*. Chris Gardner dragging his bone-density scanner across the city, attending an unpaid internship, juggling rejection with quiet dignity. He had no guarantee of a job. No assurance that it would work out. But he kept showing up because the process was the only thing within his control.

I think of J.K. Rowling — now admired across the world, but once a single mother living on government assistance. She wrote in cafés because her apartment was too cold. She scribbled ideas on scraps of paper while her daughter slept beside her.

There was no audience. No certainty. No publisher waiting.

Twelve publishers rejected *Harry Potter.*

Not softly — simply "no."

Most would have stopped long before the twelfth rejection. But Rowling kept writing because the act of writing itself sustained her. She trusted the process long before the world believed in her.

And when success arrived, it arrived like a storm — but only after years of quiet persistence.

Recently, I heard a smaller story that carried the same lesson. A woman who started a YouTube channel kept refreshing her analytics — subscribers, views, watch time — multiple times a day. Each refresh brought anxiety.

After months of frustration, she stopped obsessing over numbers and focused only on creating consistently — one honest video at a time.

Within weeks, her channel was monetised. Today she earns well and enjoys the work again.

She said something that stayed with me: "The results came when I stopped chasing them."

Isn't that how life often works?

I've seen it in ordinary stories too.

A neighbour who couldn't jog for three minutes eventually completed a half-marathon — because he showed up daily.

A baker who began with one small order a week now runs a thriving kitchen — because she kept improving quietly.

A student practised spoken English every day for a year. Confidence didn't appear overnight — but it appeared.

The world today is obsessed with outcomes. "How fast?" "How soon?" "How big?"

But speed without direction is meaningless. Direction comes from process — the slow, repetitive, unglamorous discipline that few people notice.

If you trace the journey of anyone you admire, you will always find a long stretch of invisible effort when nothing seemed to be happening.

A seed does not know it will become a tree. It simply keeps growing.

The Core Idea

Tomorrow, pick one thing you are working on — a habit, a skill, a project — and give it your full effort without checking how it's performing. Don't measure. Don't compare. Don't refresh the page. Just show up. When you stop chasing outcomes, the work becomes lighter — and the results, sooner or later, find their way to you.

PART 6

Karma, Choices & Moral Clarity

29

Don't Forget Your Hanumans

The older I grow, the more I realise that none of us succeeds alone. Even the moments in my life that looked like "my big victories" were never mine alone. Someone was always holding the ladder steady while I climbed. Someone was doing the unglamorous, unseen work so the final picture looked effortless.

A few years ago, after a particularly frantic week at work, I stood on stage receiving an award. Cameras flashed, applause echoed, and people congratulated me as though I had single-handedly pulled off a miracle.

Later that evening, back in my hotel room, I opened my inbox and found a message from one of the most dependable members of my team:

"Sir, reached home. Your presentation went well — glad the crisis didn't show."

He didn't mention that he had worked three nights straight fixing the numbers. He didn't mention the 2 a.m. call when he said, "Don't worry, I'll handle it." He didn't even stay for the ceremony. He just went home quietly.

That night, it struck me: this man was my Hanuman.

In the Ramayana, Hanuman never waits for the spotlight. He does not ask for credit. He lifts mountains silently. When he finds Sita, he does not make a grand announcement; he simply hands over Rama's ring and bows. When he burns Lanka, he does not boast later. He says only, "I did what I could."

We remember Rama's charisma. But the war was carried on Hanuman's shoulders.

In our own lives, we all have Hanumans. We just forget to notice them.

Think back to your school days. Was there a teacher who believed in you before you believed in yourself? A friend who stood by you during a phase you would rather forget?

At work, isn't there someone who takes your late-night calls, spots your errors before they go public, reminds you gently, "Sir, the meeting is at 4, not 5"?

At home, our Hanumans quietly keep life running.

The accountant friend who saves you from a tax mistake. The sibling who covers for you when you miss a family event. The house help who remembers how you like your tea. The spouse who absorbs your stress without complaint, reading your silences like a language.

They may not lift mountains of stone. But they lift emotional mountains. And that is often harder.

I have seen people rise to powerful positions and slowly forget this truth. A senior leader once said to me, "I worked hard for this. I made it alone." But when you forget your Hanumans, something inside you becomes hollow.

Not long ago, a young colleague shared something simple yet profound. He said, "Sir, my father is not expressive. But every morning, before I wake up, he fills my water bottle and keeps my bag ready. He thinks I don't notice. But I do."

That father will never stand on a stage. No spotlight will ever fall on him. Yet he is shaping a life quietly. That is devotion in its purest form.

Gratitude does not require expensive gifts or dramatic speeches. It requires memory. Remember who held your hand when others walked away. Remember who stayed awake worrying about you. Remember who pushed the boat so you could sail smoothly.

Everyone wants to be Rama.

Very few choose to be Hanuman.

The Core Idea

Tomorrow morning, think of one person who has quietly supported you — at home, at work, or in life. Send them one sincere message of gratitude. Just one. You will notice how a relationship deepens the moment you say, "I remember what you did for me. Thank you."

30

Exercise or Excuse? You Choose

Veteran comic poet Surender Sharma has a gift for distilling India's wisdom — and laziness — into a single punchline. With his trademark deadpan style, he once said: "A horse runs all its life and lives barely 20 years. But an anaconda just lies coiled up and lives thousands! So why tax your body? Anyway, if man was meant to walk everywhere, why did scientists invent cars?"

Only Surender Sharma can make laziness sound philosophical. His humour is our stress pill — the antidote to taking life too seriously. It's meant to be enjoyed with a pinch of salt. The trouble begins when we take the salt and forget the sense.

Recently, I saw a LinkedIn post that echoed something similar: "People say you should be careful about your lifestyle after 60. I would rather enjoy my drinks, smoke, and fried snacks than spend my evenings counting steps or calories. Time is short — let's live it fully!"

And then there's the social media classic: "If you replace your coffee with green tea, you'll lose 97% of what little joy you have left in life."

Funny? Absolutely. Relatable? Of course.

But also a little dangerous.

Because beneath that humour often hides surrender — the idea that growing older means giving up on yourself.

I've heard people say, "What's the point now? I've earned the right to relax." And yes, relaxation is earned. But neglect is not relaxation. It's slow self-sabotage.

Exercise may not guarantee a longer life. But it certainly adds life to your years. And it is never too late to begin.

Look at Milind Soman's mother, Usha Soman — well into her eighties — still doing push-ups and planks that would challenge people half her age. Or Ernestine Shepherd, who became the world's oldest female bodybuilder after starting at 56. Or the many "Insta grandmas" sharing yoga routines, proving age is not a barrier.

The body remains loyal — if we give it a chance.

Excuses, however, are persuasive:

"I walk enough inside the house."

"My work is mental exercise."

"My grandmother never went to a gym and she lived till 90."

But remember the lifestyle of that generation. Fresh food. Physical chores. Minimal screens. No traffic stress. Their daily life was movement. Ours is mostly sitting.

In other words, we need to do what they didn't have to.

Yes, I too have wondered: Why do some people abuse their bodies and live long, while health-conscious ones leave early? There is no perfect formula. But there is one clear truth

— health is not only about how long you live. It is about how well you live.

You may have heard this before: "When we are healthy, we think about a hundred things. When we are unwell, we think about only one."

That says it all.

Good health gives freedom — the freedom to think clearly, travel comfortably, laugh without pain, and live without constant limitation. No indulgence can replace that.

Movement has quiet magic. Even ten minutes can change your mood, your breathing, your stress levels. A walk stretches more than your legs — it stretches your mind.

Our scriptures speak of balance. The body is a temple. Movement is gratitude. The Gita reminds us of moderation and alignment. When you treat your body with respect, it rewards you with clarity.

And you don't need marathons.

A 15-minute walk.

A few stretches.

Taking the stairs.

Dancing to your favourite song.

Anything that reminds your body what it was designed to do — move.

A friend in his seventies begins each day with yoga. I once asked him how he stays consistent. He smiled and said, "I replaced discipline with devotion."

That stayed with me.

Perhaps exercise is not punishment. It is prayer. A simple way of saying thank you to a body that carries you through everything.

So whether it's yoga, cycling, walking, or pretending to be Govinda in your living room — move. You don't need a perfect plan. You just need a willing start.

The Core Idea

Tomorrow morning, before you open your phone, move your body for ten minutes. Walk. Stretch. Dance. Breathe. And when your mind whispers an excuse — and it will — smile, and move anyway. Because one day your body will ask for very little — just enough strength to do what you love. Start building that strength now.

31

Where the Water Gets In

It was the kind of night that tests both boats and people — dark, howling, unpredictable. A small family set out across a river, their boat rocking gently at first, then violently as the wind picked up. Soon the sky cracked open, and rain lashed their faces.

Then came the shout that turns calm into chaos:

"Water's coming in!"

Everyone panicked. Someone grabbed a pot, another cupped their hands, and soon the boat was full of noise — frantic scooping, worried whispers, trembling prayers. But no matter how fast they bailed, the water kept rising.

In the middle of this panic, an elderly man — the grandfather — slowly opened his eyes. He had been resting quietly, trusting the younger ones to steer. What he saw was confusion: people throwing water overboard without noticing the growing hole beneath them.

He said gently, "Stop. Before you empty the boat, find where the water is coming from."

They froze.

One of the younger boys spotted it — a hole near the edge, hidden by a loose plank shaken by the storm. The old man tore off a piece of wood, wedged it firmly into place, and motioned for them to start bailing again.

Within minutes, the water level dropped. The panic faded.

When they finally reached the other shore — tired but safe — the old man quietly said:

"First stop the inflow. Then manage the outflow."

That line stayed with me. Because life, when you think about it, works exactly the same way.

We spend so much time scooping water out of sinking situations — reacting, fixing, firefighting — that we rarely pause to ask why the problem started in the first place.

I've seen it everywhere — in offices, homes, friendships, even in my own habits. When stress builds up, we look for quick relief: a new gadget, a short vacation, another cup of coffee. We scoop and scoop, but the water keeps rising.

The wiser approach is to stop and look for the leak.

Sometimes that leak is an unhealthy routine. Sometimes it is a resentment we ignored. Sometimes it is our inability to say no.

I once found myself working twelve-hour days, convinced I was being productive, until my health began to protest. My doctor didn't prescribe stronger medicine. He simply said, "You don't need a stronger body — you need stronger boundaries."

That was my leaky boat moment.

Even in cricket you see this wisdom. Sachin Tendulkar once said he never blamed the bowler for getting him out.

Instead, he studied the delivery that dismissed him and ensured it wouldn't fool him again. He didn't just bail faster — he fixed the weakness.

In business too, the lesson repeats itself. A senior leader once told me, "We reward the firefighters. But the real heroes are the ones who quietly prevent the fire."

Preventive wisdom is rarely glamorous. It doesn't trend. It doesn't make headlines. But it is what keeps the ship afloat.

I once had a neighbour in his sixties who looked remarkably fit. When I asked him his secret, he smiled and said, "I don't diet. I don't gym. I just don't let things pile up — not dishes, not emotions, not weight."

What a beautiful way to live: fix small leaks before they become floods.

Our scriptures echo this idea too. Lord Mahavira spoke of *Samayik* — the practice of constant awareness, pausing to observe one's thoughts before they turn into harmful actions. Buddhism calls it mindfulness. Psychology calls it emotional regulation.

But the essence is simple: pause before the damage grows.

Even relationships follow this rule. I once saw two friends stop speaking for months over a small misunderstanding. When one finally reached out, the other said, "I thought you didn't care."

Unspoken words can be tiny holes. If they remain unattended, resentment slowly fills the boat.

Look at the world around us. Environmental problems, social divisions, corruption — often we treat the symptoms instead of fixing the source. We keep scooping water while the hole remains open.

The old man in the boat offered a philosophy for every storm — personal, professional, even global.

Perhaps we forget prevention because it is invisible. No one applauds the accident that never happened, the illness that never came, the argument that never began.

Yet the peace created by foresight is its own quiet reward.

So the next time chaos surrounds you, pause for a moment. Look for the hole. Fix it at the root. Then act — calmly, steadily, wisely.

The Core Idea

Tomorrow, look at one area of your life that keeps leaking energy — your health, your time, or your peace of mind. Then take one small step to plug the hole at its source. If it's your health, pause before reaching for another coffee or painkiller. Ask what your body truly needs — rest, water, or a walk. If it's your time, say no to one unnecessary task or meeting. Protect that hour like you would a lifeboat. If it's your peace of mind, stop replaying what went wrong. Write it down, forgive where possible, and let it go. Because true strength is not about bailing faster. It is about noticing where the water gets in — and calmly sealing the crack before it sinks your boat.

32

Less Is Enough

In Jain philosophy, *Gochari* is a way of life.

It refers to the daily practice of monks and nuns who go from house to house, accepting small portions of food that are freely offered. They never request a specific dish, never take more than what is given, and never collect from the same house twice in a row.

The idea is simple yet profound: take what you need, not what you desire; accept with grace, without creating burden or expectation.

The word *gochari* literally means "wandering like a cow."

Just as a cow moves gently from one door to another, nibbling a little here and a little there without exhausting any one source, a monk gathers sustenance in small, mindful portions.

Nothing is wasted, no one is burdened, and nature remains in balance.

When I first understood the depth of this practice, it struck me how perfectly it applies to modern life — even though we do not walk barefoot from door to door. Because, in a sense, we too are gatherers, collecting food, experiences, relationships, possessions, and knowledge as we move through life. Somewhere along the way, however, gathering quietly turned into hoarding.

We no longer take just enough. We take too much — from the planet, from people, and even from ourselves.

We eat beyond hunger, shop beyond need, work beyond capacity, scroll beyond purpose.

Our consumption has slowly outgrown our compassion.

A few years ago, I met a Jain monk in Shravanabelagola who explained it beautifully. He said, "We eat what is offered, not what we crave. Because craving creates karma — not in the stomach, but in the mind."

That sentence stayed with me. Because even outside religion, the truth still holds: every excess creates imbalance.

Think about it.

When we overeat, the body suffers.

When we overwork, relationships begin to strain.

When we overconsume, the planet pays.

The practice of *Gochari* reminds us to move gently — to take small portions from many doors, whether those "doors" are opportunities, pleasures, or resources.

There is a quiet grace in that approach.

When you take a little from each source, you allow everyone the chance to contribute. You keep things flowing. And you avoid the trap of greed.

I remember once visiting a friend who lived in a small village in Gujarat. His family would always cook extra chapatis for passing monks. When one monk stopped by, he accepted just half a roti, smiled warmly, and blessed the house.

My friend's mother later said, "The blessing he gave us was worth far more than the food he took."

That's the magic of taking little — it multiplies joy on both sides.

And yet, in the modern world, we've quietly come to believe that more is always better.

More money.

More recognition.

More luxury.

More followers.

But ask anyone who already has "more," and they will often admit that the craving never truly ends. Because the real hunger is not in the stomach — it is in the mind.

A related element of Jain philosophy is called *aparigraha* — non-possessiveness or non-attachment. You do not have to renounce the world; you simply loosen your grip on it.

I've met billionaires who can buy anything but still crave peace. And I've met monks who own almost nothing yet radiate joy. The difference isn't in what they possess — it's in how lightly they hold it.

Even ambition follows this law.

There is nothing wrong with wanting to succeed — but like *Gochari*, it must be practised with balance. Take a little from each source. Learn from different people. Grow steadily, but without greed.

In work, this means avoiding burnout — not squeezing yourself dry in pursuit of results.

In relationships, it means giving space — not consuming someone's emotional energy completely.

In success, it means staying grounded — not losing yourself to excess.

In the larger sense, *Gochari* becomes a mindset — a gentle reminder that every act of consumption carries responsibility.

How can we practise it in everyday life?

Take what you need from the internet — and log off.

Eat until you're satisfied, not stuffed.

Buy one good thing instead of five disposable ones.

Speak only when your words truly add value.

Use water, energy, or attention with gratitude, not entitlement.

Because ultimately, every resource — material or emotional — is borrowed.

Monks understand this instinctively. That's why they walk lightly, eat modestly, and thank the world before each bite.

For them, *Gochari* is worship — not of food, but of restraint.

And what a beautiful form of worship that is: to take only enough and leave the rest for others; to consume without depleting; to enjoy without becoming enslaved by desire.

In a way, the world itself works like this. The sun shines on all without hoarding light. Rivers flow without storing water. Trees give fruit without claiming ownership.

Everything in nature follows *Gochari* — except us.

Maybe that's why we sometimes feel restless despite abundance.

We have everything, yet we still don't know when to stop grazing.

The Core Idea

Tomorrow, try living one day in the spirit of *Gochari*. Move through your day lightly, taking only what you truly need. At the table, serve yourself a little less and eat slowly, with gratitude. Notice how "enough" feels. At work or home, choose one task and give it your full attention instead of scattering yourself across many. In speech, say only what is necessary and kind. Leave a little silence between your words. By evening, you may find a gentle calm settling in — a sense of space, balance, and quiet sufficiency.

33

The Price Is Yours

There's an old story I've loved since childhood — about Dasyu Ratnakar, the fearsome bandit who would one day become Sage Valmiki.

Ratnakar was the kind of man people whispered about in fear. He looted travellers, often killing them before taking everything they had. But when Sage Narad crossed his path one day, he neither ran nor fought. Instead, the sage asked him a single question that would change his life forever.

"Why do you commit such sins?"

Ratnakar didn't hesitate. "For my family," he said. "They depend on me."

Sage Narad nodded, then asked quietly, "Will your family share your sins too?"

Ratnakar laughed. "Of course! They enjoy what I earn; they must share the burden."

Narad simply said, "Go ask them."

So Ratnakar went home and asked his wife, his parents, his children — one by one. And each of them gave the same answer: "No. Your sins are yours alone. It is your responsibility to take care of us, but we never asked you to commit a crime."

He returned shattered. In that moment, everything he believed — loyalty, love, justification — came crashing down.

Narad did not scold him or preach. He simply said, "Then make a new start. Chant the name of Rama."

But Ratnakar found himself unable to even say it. His tongue, used to violence, stumbled over the sacred name. So Narad gently told him, "Then say *Mara*. Say it again and again."

And as he did — *Mara Mara Mara* — the syllables slowly melted into *Rama Rama Rama*. Gradually, the bandit became the sage. The sinner became the storyteller. And from his pen emerged the Ramayana.

I've often thought about this story — and how closely it mirrors our lives today.

Because, let's face it, most of us aren't robbers in the literal sense. But haven't we all, at some point, justified a wrong in the name of family, work, or necessity? It might be something small — like frequently leaving work early because "everyone else does it, and they'll stand up for me." News: yes, they might nod in agreement, but no, they won't stand with you when it matters.

Sometimes we convince ourselves that the end will justify the means. But as Ratnakar learned, it rarely works that way. You can share your salary, your home, your meals — but not your actions.

I've seen this play out in small but telling ways, and I'm sure you'll find an echo of it in your own life. Years ago, a friend of mine made a decision at work — not entirely honest, but profitable. "I did it for my team," he said proudly. "They'll benefit."

And they did — for a while.

But when the truth surfaced, no one stood by him. Not one person. He took the fall alone. For years after that, he would say quietly, "But I did this for them…"

It reminded me of Ratnakar — and the way life always returns responsibility to its rightful owner. As the saying goes, "A boon is shared; a curse is personal." Or in simpler words, "Laugh and the world laughs with you; cry and you cry alone."

Think about it.

If something good happens to you — a blessing, a stroke of luck, a moment of joy — you rush to share it. "Have sweets!" "Come celebrate!" Blessings invite company.

But when something goes wrong — guilt, regret, consequences — you bear it alone. No one stands in that fire with you. Often, you cannot even ask them to.

And while it may feel harsh, it is life's way of nudging us toward awareness. The moment you truly own your actions, something powerful happens — the same transformation that turned Ratnakar into Valmiki. The past loosens its grip.

That's the real miracle of this story — not that a bandit became a saint, but that anyone can change if they're willing to face themselves honestly.

Narad did not deliver a long lecture on morality. He simply offered a starting point — a single word: *Mara*.

It is like life whispering gently, "Start where you are. You don't have to be perfect. Just begin."

You might have heard the old saying, "When the ship starts to sink, the rats are the first to leave."

It sounds crude, but it carries a truth — and not just about ships.

When things are going well — when money flows and success shines — people gather. But when trouble arrives, when the truth begins to surface, even the closest ones quietly step away.

We've seen it happen many times. When Harshad Mehta's empire began to crumble, the same people who once celebrated him as a financial genius stopped taking his calls. When a powerful politician or celebrity faces scandal, their inner circle suddenly grows smaller. The smiles fade. The phones fall silent.

That's what karma does. It strips away illusion and leaves you face to face with your own actions.

A boon draws people closer; a curse isolates. When you act with integrity, others are willing to stand beside you. But when your choices are tainted, even your own shadow begins to feel heavier.

And that is what Dasyu Ratnakar discovered too. When he went home and asked if his family would share his sins, they all said no. His ship had begun to sink — and the comforts he relied on quietly disappeared, leaving him alone with his conscience.

But that is also the beauty of the story — when everything else falls away, you finally meet yourself.

The Core Idea

Tonight, take a quiet moment and ask yourself: Is there something I'm justifying in the name of love, duty, or work — that my conscience doesn't fully agree with? You don't need to fix everything at once. Just acknowledge it. That's where the healing begins. Because the story of Valmiki isn't only about sin and salvation — it's about courage. The courage to face yourself. The courage to begin again. And remember: blessings multiply when shared, but burdens lighten only when owned.

34

The Circle Always Closes

Lord Mahavira once stood deep in meditation in a quiet forest. A cowherd approached him and asked if he would watch over his oxen while he went to the nearby village. Mahavira, absorbed in stillness, gave no response.

When the cowherd returned, his animals were gone. Furious, he shouted at Mahavira, but the sage remained unmoved. In a moment of blind anger, the cowherd picked up thorn-like nails and drove them into Mahavira's ears.

It is difficult to imagine such cruelty inflicted upon an enlightened being. Yet Jain texts tell us something remarkable: this was the return of an old debt. In a previous life, Mahavira had been King Vasudeva, who once ordered molten lead to be poured into a servant's ears for disturbing his rest.

Centuries later, the pain found its way back, not as punishment, but as balance.

What does this tell us?

It reminds us that karma is the mirror we cannot avoid. What we do, how we speak, what we think — it all circles back until balance is restored.

Even an enlightened soul like Mahavira was not exempt from it. And if that is true for him, what might it mean for the rest of us?

It means that every word, every act, every thought carries weight. When we hurt someone, even unintentionally, that energy does not simply disappear. It travels, lingers, and eventually returns. And when we choose kindness, the same law quietly applies. It too finds its way back, often when we need it most.

You see, karma is not some distant or abstract concept. It is unfolding around us every day — sometimes quietly, sometimes in ways that feel almost extraordinary.

One of my favourite modern examples is the story of Alexander Fleming, the Scottish doctor who discovered penicillin in 1928. Long before that, as a young man, he once saved a wealthy boy from drowning in a bog. The boy's father, grateful for the rescue, offered to pay for Fleming's education. Years later, Fleming's discovery of penicillin saved millions of lives — including Winston Churchill, who was that very boy he had rescued decades earlier.

Coincidence? Perhaps. But if you believe in karma, it feels like something far more profound — a kindness finding its way back home.

I have also seen it in smaller ways, and I suspect you have too. A stranger offering help at the exact moment you need it. A door opening after you have helped someone without expecting anything in return. Even the timing of a setback.

Often, what first appears to be misfortune turns out to be a quiet course correction we did not realise we needed.

Karma is not about revenge, nor is it about reward. It is about rhythm.

Every religion expresses this idea in its own language. The Bhagavad Gita says, "As you act, so shall you become." The Bible reminds us, "A man reaps what he sows." The Quran declares, "Whoever does an atom's weight of good shall see it." And Jainism adds a beautiful insight: every action binds the soul, and only awareness can release it.

That is why the practice of *pratikraman* — daily reflection and forgiveness — lies at the heart of Jain philosophy. It is a simple yet profound ritual of looking inward at the end of each day and asking yourself:

"Did I hurt anyone today — even through a careless word or thought?"

Whenever I ask myself that question, the answer is almost always yes. Sometimes it is an impatient tone with someone I love. Sometimes it is a dismissive remark I did not intend. Sometimes it is simply indifference when I could have chosen kindness.

Yet the moment I acknowledge it, something shifts inside me. The awareness softens me. It reminds me, quietly but firmly, to do better tomorrow.

That, to me, is karma. Not the cosmic scoreboard we sometimes fear, but a daily opportunity to restore balance.

People often ask me, "But what about those who do wrong and still seem to get ahead?"

I have wondered that myself. And over the years, I have met quite a few of them — people who bent the rules, played politics, or quietly took credit for work they did not do. By most worldly measures, many of them appear successful. They have the homes, the cars, the recognition.

But when you meet them in private, the story often sounds different. Some have admitted to feeling restless, even deeply lonely. They speak about sleepless nights and about how guilt creeps in quietly once the noise of the day fades away. No amount of wealth or comfort seems able to silence that voice entirely.

And perhaps that, too, is karma. Because success and peace are not the same thing. You can outrun many things in life — deadlines, people, even your own conscience — but as someone once said with a smile, "You cannot escape taxes and karma."

Even our mythology reflects this idea through stories of rebirth — kings returning as slaves, villains as reptiles. These are poetic reminders that life eventually lets us experience both sides of the equation. We hurt, and we are hurt. We love, and we are loved in return.

The beautiful thing about karma is that it can be repaired. Right here, right now, you can begin building better karma. A sincere apology can dissolve years of bitterness. A small act of generosity can ripple outward into unseen blessings.

So the real question is not "Will I face my karma?" but rather, "What am I creating right now?"

Karma is not cruel. It is corrective. It is humbling to realise that even Mahavira was not exempt from it. But it is also deeply comforting, because it means none of us are beyond redemption.

In today's world, reflecting on karma feels more relevant than ever. A rude message, a dishonest post, a harsh word — they can come back almost instantly. What once took lifetimes now seems to circle back within days.

Because whether we realise it or not, every choice is planting something.

The Core Idea

Tonight, before you sleep, sit quietly for a minute. Think about the day that has just passed. Did your words, your actions, or even your silence cause hurt? If the answer is yes, whisper a quiet "I'm sorry." If not, whisper "Thank you." That small moment of reflection, done sincerely, is karma's quiet antidote. Because in the end, what we place into the world always finds its way back to us.

35

The Poison of Assumptions

The other day, I was having a long, intense conversation with a friend I've known for over two decades. We were talking about how easily people form opinions these days — about others, about situations, even about things they barely understand.

So I asked him a question.

"Imagine this," I said. "Suppose we don't meet for a month. During that time, a few of our mutual friends begin saying unpleasant things about me. They all tell you the same story — the same words, the same tone. Would you still wait to ask me my side, or would a part of you start believing them? Be honest."

He paused for a moment. Then he said, "I suppose I might start believing them. It's strange, isn't it?"

It is — and yet it's something we all fall for.

I've seen it happen in offices, families, friendships — even in society at large. Someone says something unkind, someone else repeats it, and soon a small whisper grows into a full-blown narrative. Before long, we are judging, labelling, and deciding — all based on fragments of something someone said.

Over the years, I've reflected on why that happens, and I think it comes down to a few uncomfortable truths.

We remember the one mistake more easily than the hundred good deeds.

A lie, when repeated often enough, begins to sound like the truth.

And while truth walks slowly, lies travel at lightning speed.

The truth also has a difficult job. It needs proof. It requires patience, evidence, and sometimes courage. Lies, on the other hand, arrive dressed as confidence. They come polished and ready to be believed. Lies also have cheerleaders — people with small agendas, insecurities, or simply boredom to fill. The truth often stands alone.

But can this pattern ever be reversed?

I believe it can — if we begin where all revolutions truly start: within the mind.

We need to create a kind of mental firewall, one that stops unverified words from entering our system. Before we react, repeat, or believe, we must pause and ask a simple question: Do I know this to be true?

There's a beautiful old metaphor from Indian philosophy — the swan that can separate milk from water. *Neer-Ksheer Vivek*: the discernment (*vivek*) to separate water (*neer*) from milk (*ksheer*).

It comes from the ancient belief that the *rajhans* — the royal swan — possesses the mythical ability to drink only the milk from a mixture of milk and water, leaving the water behind.

Just like that swan, the wise learn to separate fact from gossip, intention from noise. They do not consume everything that comes their way.

In today's world of instant messaging and instant outrage, this ability is more valuable than ever. You know only too well how easily reputations can be maligned, and how quickly we react before we reflect.

But I've learned — sometimes through personal experience — that most people who get swept away by gossip or falsehoods are not bad people. They are simply busy and distracted, just like you and me. And that is why the real battle is not between truth and lies; it is between attention and assumption.

One of the most powerful reminders of this came from my own life. Years ago, at work, a rumour circulated about a decision I had supposedly made. It was completely untrue. Yet by the time I heard about it, the story had already travelled across departments.

My instinct was to defend myself immediately — to explain, to prove, to correct the record. But instead, I waited. Perhaps because I was too hurt to respond right away, or perhaps because I instinctively believed that truth does not need a megaphone. Whatever the reason, my silence served me well. The facts surfaced in time, and those who had doubted me eventually saw the reality for themselves.

Since then, I've tried to handle such moments differently. When someone tells me something negative about another person, I ask a simple question: "Did you hear it from them directly?" Most of the time, the answer is no. And that is usually where the conversation ends.

It is a small habit, but it filters out a surprising amount of unnecessary negativity.

The great spiritual texts remind us of this principle as well. The Bhagavad Gita warns against gossip and harsh speech as poisons of the tongue. The Bible advises, "Let every man be swift to hear, slow to speak, slow to anger." The Quran reminds us, "If a wicked person comes to you with news, verify it."

Different words, the same timeless truth: integrity begins with how we listen.

So how do we purify this "poison of opinion"?

By trusting wisely, not blindly. By questioning without cynicism. By learning to hold our judgments lightly until we truly know.

The real antidote to opinion is curiosity. The moment you choose to ask rather than assume, something shifts. You move from being part of the noise to becoming part of the understanding.

Imagine a world where we gave each other that benefit of the doubt — where we paused before forwarding a message, repeating a rumour, or forming a verdict. It would not make us naïve. It would make us humane.

Because in the end, building a beautiful world is a collective effort. And truth is its foundation. To build that foundation well, we must first make sure the poison of assumption loses its power.

The Core Idea

Tomorrow, when you hear something about someone — a colleague, a friend, even a public figure — pause before believing or reacting. Ask yourself a simple question: Do I know this for certain? And if the answer is no, choose silence over speculation. In doing so, you help build a world rooted in truth.

36

Ek Ruka Hua Faisla (A Pending Decision)

Twelve jurors sit in a room, locked in a heated debate over a murder trial. Eleven of them are convinced the accused is guilty, but one man refuses to conform. He insists there is room for doubt — that the boy on trial deserves a fair hearing before being condemned.

What follows is an extraordinary exchange of logic, empathy, and patience. In that small, stuffy room, without a single scene change or background score, one man's quiet conviction slowly transforms anger into understanding. By the end, every juror changes his mind — from guilt to innocence.

Ek Ruka Hua Faisla (originally *Twelve Angry Men*) has stayed with me for years. Every time I watch it, I find myself discovering something new — not about the film, but about myself.

It taught me that decision-making is not about authority or speed. It is about understanding. It is about creating the space where truth can breathe.

At work, I have often found myself in situations that feel remarkably similar to that jurors' room — high-stakes discussions, tight timelines, differing opinions, and a room full of people trying to be heard.

During one project, despite having all the necessary resources, a particular state office was struggling to deliver results. Deadlines were being missed, and frustration was steadily building on both sides — at headquarters and within the ground team.

Instead of sending yet another round of emails or reports, we decided to visit in person. Senior functional leaders from HQ joined me, and we brought together all the state leaders and their teams in one room. Titles, hierarchies, and formalities were deliberately set aside. The goal was simple: let's talk.

Each person was given the opportunity to speak openly about what was not working — not as a complaint, but as an observation. Some issues turned out to be as simple as pending approvals from HQ. Others were coordination gaps between functions. Gradually, the mood in the room began to shift as people realised they were being heard rather than judged.

We did not stop when lunchtime arrived. Food was ordered into the room, turning the meeting into a working lunch, and the conversation continued. By the end of the day, we had clear action points, defined responsibilities, and — most importantly — a shared sense of ownership. A small monitoring team was set up to track progress and timelines.

The result was remarkable. The long-pending project, which had dragged on for months, was completed ahead of schedule. The APEX team appreciated the effort, but what pleased me most was that the credit went to the people on the ground — the last line of execution. They were the real heroes.

That experience reinforced what *Ek Ruka Hua Faisla* had taught me years earlier: real change begins when people feel heard.

Over time, I also came to understand why this approach worked so effectively.

1. Teamwork over Individual Effort

No single person can execute a project alone. It requires cooperation, coordination, and the willingness to step beyond silos. A chain is only as strong as its weakest link, and the best leaders strengthen those links — not through blame, but through belief.

2. The Power of Open Dialogue

A breakthrough idea can come from anywhere — a junior associate, a field officer, even a temporary staff member. The juror in *Ek Ruka Hua Faisla* was not the loudest voice; he was the most patient listener. When people feel safe enough to speak, ideas that once remained hidden beneath fear or hesitation begin to surface.

3. Breaking the "Silos" Mentality

In many organisations, individuals begin protecting their territories. Gradually, ambition overshadows purpose. The focus shifts from "How do we succeed?" to "How do I look successful?" And that is often when teams begin to weaken.

Rewarding only those in the spotlight is like watering just one branch of a tree. It may appear green for a while, but the rest slowly begins to dry out. True success comes when every contributor — visible or invisible — feels valued.

That is why I began adopting what I call the *Jury Room Approach*: one room, honest voices, no rank. It is remarkable how much clarity emerges when formality is replaced with trust.

But beyond the corporate results, this method changed me personally. It made me realise that listening is not merely a soft skill — it is a superpower. We often rush to conclusions because silence feels uncomfortable. We mistake decisiveness for wisdom. Yet, as the film quietly shows, sometimes leadership means being the one who pauses and says, "Let's think again."

I have tried to carry this lesson into other parts of life as well. Whether it is a family disagreement or a community issue, the principle remains the same: people do not necessarily want instant solutions — they want to feel understood. And once that happens, half the problem often resolves itself.

Cinema, when done well, holds up a mirror to life. *Ek Ruka Hua Faisla* did that for me. It reminded me that truth often hides in plain sight — but we only see it when we slow down enough to look.

The film ends with no celebration, no applause — just quiet understanding. That is often how good decisions are made too. Not in noise, but in clarity.

The Core Idea

The next time you find yourself in a group discussion — at work or at home — try the *Jury Room Approach.* Step back. Listen fully before speaking. Ask questions not to challenge, but to understand. Invite every voice into the conversation, especially the quieter ones. Because the best decisions are not made by the loudest voices. They are made by the ones who care enough to listen.

PART 7

Faith, Growth & the Long View

37

Many Paths, One Light

During my years in Haridwar, my mornings began at 4:30 a.m. This sacred hour, when the world holds its breath between night and dawn, is described as *Amrit Bela* in several traditions. I could feel its sanctity in my very soul. The Ganga flowed quietly outside, the birds had not yet begun their songs, and the stillness felt almost alive. In that silence, words took on a new life. They felt gentle, luminous, and full of meaning.

Being an avid seeker of wisdom, I chose to fill this hour with reading. I began with the *Bhagavad Gita*, then moved on to the *Ramayana* and *Ramcharitmanas*. My curiosity eventually led me to the Jain *Agamas*. I wanted to understand whether the belief we carry, that our own religion or path is somehow supreme, comes from truth or simply from habit and inheritance. I wanted to see whether faith, when stripped of language and geography, still spoke the same truth. So I turned to the Bible and the Quran as well.

The deeper I went, the more I realised that every religion carries its wisdom not only in sermons or rituals, but in the rhythm of daily life. Each faith has built-in reminders that guide us toward humility, health, and kindness. These reminders often appear not in grand declarations, but in simple, everyday acts.

Take fasting, for instance. Almost every major religion prescribes it, not as punishment but as purification. Muslims observe *Roza* during Ramadan, practising restraint, patience, and gratitude. Jains fast during *Paryushan* to cleanse both body and mind. Hindus observe fasts such as *Ekadashi*, and Christians fast during Lent. The forms differ, but the essence remains the same. When we give the body less, we often give the spirit more space to grow.

Food itself is treated with reverence across traditions. The Bible cautions, "Do not destroy the work of God for the sake of food." The Quran warns against excess and urges moderation and thankfulness. In Jainism, the act of eating is almost a meditation, reminding us to consume with awareness, restraint, and gratitude, while causing the least possible harm. Across religions, food is not merely nourishment. It is awareness in action.

Every religion also teaches us how to begin the day, quietly and consciously, before the world fully awakens. The Gayatri Mantra in Hinduism invokes divine light at dawn. Muslims rise for the Fajr prayer. Christians begin their mornings with devotion and reflection. Jain monks practise *samayik*, centring themselves in stillness and mindfulness. The languages and rituals differ, but each tradition asks the same thing of us: begin the day with purpose, humility, and presence.

Even clothing and cleanliness, which are sometimes dismissed as mere ritual, carry deep psychological meaning.

The Quran speaks of modesty and cleanliness as acts of faith. Hindu scriptures describe wearing fresh, simple clothes and bathing at sunrise to honour the divine within. Jain monks wear unstitched white cloth to symbolise purity, simplicity, and detachment. Each tradition, in its own way, reminds us that discipline on the outside often nurtures calm within.

Then there is silence, a virtue that almost every faith considers sacred. Jainism teaches *maun*, the discipline of mindful speech and deliberate silence. The Bible advises, "Be quick to listen, slow to speak." The Quran teaches, "Speak what is good, or remain silent." What all three traditions recognise is that words carry weight, and that silence, when chosen wisely, often heals more than argument ever can.

As I continued reading, I began to notice deeper parallels. The *Bhagavad Gita* teaches, "Do your duty without attachment to the result." The Bible echoes a similar wisdom: "Lay not up for yourselves treasures on earth." The *Agamas* add, "He who conquers desire conquers sorrow." Three different texts, yet one clear insight: peace begins where greed and attachment begin to loosen their hold.

Forgiveness too finds common ground across traditions. Jesus said, "Forgive them, for they know not what they do." Lord Mahavira taught, "Forgive all living beings, and may all forgive me." The Quran praises those "who pardon men, for God loves the doers of good." Different teachers, different eras, yet the same moral compass guiding human conduct.

Even seasonal cleansing, which many of us treat simply as cultural tradition, carries deep spiritual logic. The Hindu fasts of Navratri, the Jain observances during Paryushan, and the Christian season of Lent all coincide with seasonal shifts.

These periods gently guide the body toward renewal while reminding the mind to return to balance and self-discipline. Ancient wisdom had long understood what modern science increasingly confirms: physical discipline and spiritual clarity often strengthen each other.

These teachings are not about ritual perfection. They are about balance. Every faith, in its own way, offers a guide for harmony between mind and body, self and society, and the human and the divine. Their details differ, but their intention is remarkably similar.

The more I read, the clearer it became that the same values shine through every scripture: compassion, restraint, humility, and faith in something greater than ourselves. Religions are not identical, but they resemble different languages telling the same story.

When I finally turned to the Jain *Agamas* at the age of forty-five, it felt like coming home, but with a wider and more understanding heart. I could now read them not as the only truth, but as one beautiful expression of truth. I began to notice how naturally the teachings of Lord Mahavira resonated with those of Krishna, Christ, and the Buddha. The *Uttaradhyayana Sutra* says, "Fight with yourself; why fight with external foes?" The *Gita* echoes a similar idea: "The self is the friend and the enemy of the self." The connection was unmistakable.

Reading across religions did not dilute my faith. If anything, it deepened it. It reminded me that divinity is not confined to temples, churches, or mosques. It reveals itself in acts of sincerity, in moments of awareness, and in every quiet effort to become better than we were yesterday.

At 4:30 each morning, when the world is still half-asleep, I still sit with those scriptures. Some days it is the *Gita*. Some days it is the *Agamas*. Sometimes it is a passage from the Bible. I no longer read to compare. I read to connect. To remind myself that truth may wear many robes, but the light beneath them is the same.

The Core Idea

Tomorrow morning, take five minutes to read something from a faith that is not your own. It could be a verse, a prayer, or even a line of poetry. You do not have to agree with it. Just remain open. Notice what feels familiar, what feels compassionate, what feels true. You may discover, as I did, that wisdom does not belong to any single book or belief. It flows through all of them. Different lamps, one flame.

38

Meet Your Five Gurus

In India, we hold immense reverence for the word *Guru*. We associate it with wisdom, guidance, and awakening, someone who leads us from darkness (*gu*) to light (*ru*). But over the years, I have realised that our Gurus do not always appear in flowing robes or sit on spiritual thrones. They come in many different forms, often quietly and sometimes unrecognised.

When I look back at my own life, I can clearly see five Gurus who have shaped my journey, each arriving when I needed them the most.

1. The Light-Bringers: Our Parents

The first Guru greets us the moment we open our eyes. Parents, or whoever raises us, become our first connection to love, safety, and belonging. They introduce us to the world and, in many ways, to light itself.

I still remember holding my daughter for the first time. Her tiny fingers curled around mine, her eyes blinking against the bright hospital light. In that moment, I understood how much responsibility is carried inside that one word: parent. They are the first to show us the world, to feed us, teach us, protect us, and comfort us.

And yet, as we grow older, we often begin to take them for granted. We forget that their guidance did not end when we learned to walk or speak. It simply changed form. Even when they fall silent, their lessons remain within us: patience, resilience, kindness. Parents are our first Gurus, and often the ones we fully understand only much later in life.

2. The Torchbearers: Our Teachers

The second Guru comes in the form of teachers, those who give us knowledge, yes, but also discipline, curiosity, and the courage to think for ourselves.

I had a maths teacher in school who refused to let me give up. Whenever I complained that a problem was "too hard," she would smile and say, "Then it is worth doing." That small sentence stayed with me far longer than the equations themselves.

Another teacher helped draw me out of my shell during the years when I struggled to speak English. His faith in my ability played a huge role in building my confidence. True teachers do far more than explain grammar or solve equations. They help shape our character. They equip us with tools not just to earn a living, but to live a meaningful life.

We encounter such teachers at many stages: in school, in college, and sometimes later in life in the form of mentors, coaches, or even a wise colleague who shows us a better way to approach our work. They may not always stand at a blackboard, but each one carries a torch that lights our path.

3. The Shapers: Our Bosses and Mentors

The third Guru is the one we rarely acknowledge: our bosses, leaders, and professional mentors. They push us, challenge us, and sometimes frustrate us, but they also help bring out a version of ourselves we did not know existed.

Among the most valuable lessons I learned from one of my mentors was this: "Do not aim to be the smartest person in the room. Aim to be the most dependable." That advice became my professional compass. I take pride in being known as the person who will deliver, no matter what. *Ye kar lega* (he will get it done). Much of that confidence comes from the trust my bosses have placed in me over the years.

As a boss myself, I often have to correct or even reprimand my staff. But it is always done with the intention of helping them grow into better professionals and better human beings. This is why I say: value your workplace Gurus. They come in many forms. It may be the boss who corrects you harshly but fairly, the colleague who teaches humility through example, or the team member who reminds you to laugh even during stressful moments. In their own way, each of them shapes our craft, our ethics, and our sense of self-worth.

4. The Illuminators: Our Spiritual Guides

Then comes the fourth Guru, the one who gently turns us inward. This Guru may appear as a saint, a book, a conversation, or even a stranger who says something that quietly shifts your perspective.

Throughout my life, I have been fortunate to receive guidance from many such sources, with the *Bhagavad Gita* often serving as the fountainhead. But wisdom sometimes appears in the most unexpected places. I remember a flight during which a fellow passenger mentioned that he begins his day with twenty minutes of silence. When I asked if it was meditation, he smiled and said, "No. I started after a health scare. It is not prayer or meditation. It is simply remembering to breathe."

That small conversation stayed with me. A spiritual Guru does not always give elaborate teachings. Sometimes they simply help us see life differently. They shift our perspective of the world and, in doing so, help us understand ourselves more clearly.

5. The Silent Guru: The Self

And finally, there is the fifth and ultimate Guru, the one who lives within us.

This is the quiet voice that whispers when we are confused, the intuition that nudges us toward what feels right. It is the wisdom of all the other Gurus combined, parents, teachers, mentors, and guides, distilled into an inner awareness.

It takes time to hear this Guru clearly. For many of us, that inner voice gets drowned out by fear, ego, and the constant noise of the world. But once we begin to listen, we realise it has been there all along, patiently waiting.

This Guru asks for no rituals or grand displays of reverence. It asks only for honesty. It asks a simple question: Are you living in alignment with what you know is true? When we begin to answer that question sincerely, the search outside begins to fade. Life slowly starts to flow from the inside out.

From Darkness to Light

The beauty of these five Gurus is that they do not compete with each other. They complete each other.

Parents give us life.

Teachers give us knowledge.

Bosses give us discipline.

Spiritual guides give us awareness.

And the Self gives us peace.

Each one is a step on the ladder. Together, they help carry us from darkness to light, from dependence to independence, from confusion to clarity.

And when we finally connect with the fifth Guru within, we realise something profound: all the others were quietly preparing us to find this one.

The Core Idea

Take a moment today to remember your five Gurus, the ones who shaped you, challenged you, and guided you. Call your parents. Thank a teacher. Message an old boss. Sit quietly for a few minutes and listen to your inner voice. The journey from darkness to light is never walked alone. It is illuminated by many hands and, if you are fortunate, by the quiet wisdom of your own heart.

39

What's Your Next First

A lion hunts, catches its prey, eats, and rests until hunger calls again. Its routine remains unchanged throughout its life.

But humans are different. We grow restless with monotony. We cannot remain in the same place for too long. We crave exploration, invention, and even the possibility of failure along the way.

That, perhaps, is what makes us human. We are wired not just to survive, but to discover.

Think about the moments in your life that brought you the most happiness.

You changed your car as soon as you realised the newer model had features your old one didn't.

You switched jobs when the old one became too predictable.

You tossed out clothes that still fit perfectly well, not because they were worn out, but because they had been worn too often.

We chase newness instinctively, even when we do not fully understand why. It is our way of saying, *I want to feel alive again.*

But as life grows busier, that instinct begins to fade. We start valuing stability over surprise and certainty over curiosity. Slowly, without noticing, we forget that "first times" are not just for the young. They are for anyone who refuses to go numb.

A friend of mine took his first art class at sixty-two. Later he told me, "I realised I've been postponing joy for decades, waiting until I had time. But time doesn't arrive. You make it."

His first sketch was not great, but the sparkle in his eyes certainly was. There was something about the way he said it that felt light and free, almost childlike. He reminded me that firsts do not belong to the young. They belong to the curious.

It made me reflect on how easily we stop trying new things. Somewhere between responsibilities, deadlines, and the pursuit of stability, we quietly forget what it feels like to begin.

We start believing that firsts are meant for youth: the first job, the first love, the first adventure. But that is one of adulthood's greatest illusions. Life does not care how old you are, what title you hold, or how late you begin. The ability to start again, to say, "I have never done this before, but I will try," is what keeps us alive inside.

In fact, some of the most meaningful firsts happen much later in life. A grandparent meeting their first grandchild. A woman publishing her first book at seventy. A man learning to dance after retirement because his wife always wanted to. These are not just milestones. They are quiet celebrations of courage.

Even in our ancient stories, the theme of renewal runs deep. Arjuna, the great warrior of the Mahabharata, faced his own "first" when he froze on the battlefield, unsure and afraid. His rebirth as a warrior came not from victory, but from surrender. By listening to Krishna's wisdom, he rediscovered his purpose.

Or consider Valmiki, the sage who gave us the Ramayana. He began life as a bandit. His transformation did not come in youth but through reflection and awakening. His true "first" was not about conquest, but about consciousness.

History and creativity tell the same story again and again: it is never too late to begin. Colonel Sanders founded KFC at sixty-five. Laura Ingalls Wilder published her first *Little House* book at sixty-four. Rabindranath Tagore began painting in his seventies. Each of them started not because they suddenly had time, but because they still had the desire to feel alive.

Closer to home, I have seen quieter firsts that never make headlines. A seventy-year-old father learning to use WhatsApp just to send good morning messages to his friends. A woman who returns to singing lessons after decades. A man who finally takes a solo trip at fifty because he never found the opportunity earlier.

Each of these firsts is a small rebellion against stagnation. They remind us that the human spirit does not truly crave comfort as much as it craves renewal.

It is easy to assume that the thrill of discovery fades with age, but it does not. What fades is our willingness to step outside the familiar. We stop giving ourselves permission to be beginners. Yet being a beginner is one of life's most powerful positions. It keeps you humble, curious, and awake.

And the truth is, every single day is a first.

Every morning, I have the same quiet dialogue with myself: *You have never lived this day before. You have never seen this sunrise, felt this exact mood, or faced this particular combination of possibilities.* Each morning brings a gentle invitation: *What one new thing will you try today?*

After a certain age, the joy of firsts becomes even more meaningful than the excitement we experienced in youth. When we try something new, we feel young again. We feel alive, curious, and hopeful. And is that not the best, perhaps the only, way to live a fulfilling life?

I often think back to my friend's art class. That shaky sketch, those uncertain lines, were proof that joy still lives in trying.

The Core Idea

Tomorrow, seek out one small "first." It could be as simple as cooking or tasting a new food, taking a different route to work, or trying a new app. Allow yourself to feel that spark of discovery again, that brief moment of being a little lost and a little thrilled. Because life does not lose its magic as you grow older. You simply have to keep discovering it, again and again.

40

Smile: Life's Emotional Protein

Every morning, when my wife and I go for our walk, there's a moment that never fails to amuse her. I'll smile at someone — a stranger, a street vendor, a jogger passing by — and she'll immediately ask, "Who was that?"

And almost every time, my answer is the same: "No idea."

For me, smiling has become second nature. It's not about recognition; it's about connection. Some people smile back, some don't, but that doesn't matter. I've already earned my reward: that instant surge of warmth that feels like sunshine breaking through a cloudy morning.

I didn't always think of it this way, though. For years, I smiled simply because it felt polite — a basic social reflex. But over time, I realised it's much more than that. A genuine smile is like emotional protein, invisible nourishment for the mind and heart.

Science supports this idea. Studies show that a smile, even a forced one, sets off a chain reaction inside you. The muscles in your face send signals to the brain, triggering the release of endorphins — those feel-good chemicals that lift your mood. The brain, in turn, sends a reassuring message to the body: *You're okay. You can relax.*

It becomes a self-sustaining loop: you smile, you feel better, and that makes it easier to smile again. When someone returns that smile, the joy multiplies.

It sounds simple, almost trivial, but the impact can be profound. I remember once being at an airport after a long and chaotic day. Everyone looked tired and irritable. A young man at the security counter seemed particularly overwhelmed, juggling passengers, paperwork, and a malfunctioning scanner. When it was my turn, I handed him my boarding pass and simply smiled. For a moment he looked surprised, then he smiled back. "Thank you, sir," he said quietly.

That small exchange changed the energy of the interaction completely, for him and for me. We often underestimate how much power there is in one simple human smile.

A few years ago, I came across a quote by the Dalai Lama: "A simple smile. That's the start of opening your heart and being compassionate to others." It stayed with me. Because compassion does not always require grand gestures. Sometimes it begins with something as effortless as a smile shared on a morning walk.

Of course, there are days when smiling feels difficult. When bad news weighs heavily, when harsh words sting, or when everything seems to go wrong. On those days, I lean on what psychologists call the "facial feedback" effect. I fake it. I force a small smile, even when I don't feel like it. And somehow, it works.

The brain does not always distinguish between a real and a forced smile. It simply registers the signal and releases the same feel-good chemicals. Slowly, the heaviness begins to lift.

It's almost like gently tricking yourself into optimism — but in the best possible way.

I've also noticed that smiling changes how others respond to you. A smile disarms suspicion, builds warmth, and creates a bridge faster than words ever could. It's one reason good leaders smile — not to charm, but to reassure. It sends a subtle message: *Main hoon na* ("I'm here"). You can trust me.

There's a reason children smile nearly 400 times a day, while adults average fewer than 20. Somewhere along the way, we begin guarding our emotions as if happiness must be earned. We smile less because we're waiting for life to give us a reason.

But perhaps it works the other way around. Maybe life begins smiling back when we smile first.

It may sound sentimental, but I've seen this play out even in boardrooms. Tense meetings soften when someone walks in with genuine warmth. Disagreements turn into conversations when they begin with a friendly expression instead of a frown. The atmosphere shifts. People feel acknowledged.

And the best part is that smiling costs nothing. It's the one gift that replenishes itself every time you give it away.

I often think of it as life's emotional protein, something that strengthens your mental immunity. Just as food nourishes the body, a smile nourishes the spirit.

There's another dimension to it as well: gratitude. Every smile you share is a quiet thank-you to the world around you. It says, without words, "I see you. I acknowledge you. I'm glad to be here." In a time when most people are buried in screens or headlines, that small act becomes almost radical.

The world could use more of that right now. Not forced cheerfulness, but genuine warmth.

So the next time you're out walking, standing in line at a shop, or waiting in traffic, try it. Smile at someone. You don't need to know them, and you don't need to expect anything in return. You might just brighten both your days.

And if they don't smile back, that's perfectly fine too. You've already done your part.

The Core Idea

Tomorrow, observe your own "Smiling More Day." Try smiling at three strangers: the shopkeeper, the security guard, or the driver who lets you pass. Notice how it feels. Notice how people respond. You may not see it immediately, but each smile plants a small seed of kindness in the world — and somehow, it has a way of coming back to you when you least expect it.

41

The Happiest Man on Earth

During the long, uncertain days of the COVID-19 lockdown, like most people, I often felt trapped between worry and restlessness. The world seemed to have paused, and with it, so had we. Work shifted home, cities fell silent, and the daily headlines reminded us just how fragile life really is.

It was during those weeks that I often thought of Dhirubhai Ambani's words: "Pursue your goals even in difficulties and convert adversity into opportunity." At the time, I had mostly understood this in a business sense: adapt, innovate, stay resilient. But in the quiet isolation of those months, I began to realise its deeper meaning. Adversity, if faced with the right spirit, can become a classroom for life itself.

Around that time, my daughter gifted me a book, *The Happiest Man on Earth* by Eddie Jaku. She said, "You'll love this one. It's about gratitude." I smiled politely.

By the time I finished the first few chapters, I felt humbled.

Eddie Jaku's story is one of those rare ones that stays with you long after you close the book. A German Jew who survived the unimaginable horrors of the Holocaust, Eddie lived through imprisonment in Buchenwald and Auschwitz. He endured hunger, humiliation, loss, and suffering that defies comprehension. He escaped a death march, rebuilt his life from nothing, and eventually lived past a hundred years, calling himself the happiest man on earth.

Reading his story during a global crisis felt like holding a mirror to my own discomforts and realising how small they were.

What struck me most was not merely his survival, but his spirit. Eddie refused to let hatred or bitterness define him. Instead, he chose kindness. He wrote, "Happiness is the only thing that multiplies when you share it."

That line stayed with me.

It reminded me how often we measure success in numbers: wealth, status, achievements. Yet the richest people are often those who find joy in giving. Eddie lost everything, his family, his home, his freedom, yet he found purpose in rebuilding, in helping others, and in smiling through pain. It made me reflect that perhaps true wealth is simply the ability to remain kind even when the world is cruel.

Another lesson that resonated deeply with me was his approach to hardship. He often said, "Tomorrow will come, if you live one day at a time."

That became my quiet mantra during the pandemic. There was a time when planning even a week ahead felt impossible. So I began taking each day as it came, focusing on small routines, small wins, and small acts of normalcy. It did not remove the uncertainty, but it made life feel lighter. Sometimes endurance is not about seeing the entire road ahead; it is about believing that the next step will appear when you take this one.

Eddie also believed deeply in the power of friendship. “Without friends,” he wrote, “we are lost.” During the lockdown, I saw how true that was. From video calls to simple messages, it was our web of connections that kept many of us afloat. The people who checked in, who made you laugh, who shared the same small anxieties, reminded us that even in isolation, we were not alone.

Another passage from Eddie’s reflections made me pause. He described the human body as “the greatest machine ever built.” It made me realise how casually we take our bodies for granted, the way they heal, adapt, and endure. During COVID, when health suddenly became the centre of every conversation, that observation felt almost prophetic. Gratitude for our breath, our heartbeat, and our resilience may sound simple, but it shifts perspective in a powerful way.

But perhaps Eddie’s most profound message was this: happiness is not something the world gives you; it is something you choose to create.

He lost nearly everything, yet he still chose happiness. He said, “Where there is despair, there is misery. Where there is hope, there is happiness.”

That line changed how I thought about hope. For Eddie, hope was an act of defiance. To wake up after a day of suffering and still believe in tomorrow is hope in its purest form.

I realised that Eddie Jaku did something even more remarkable than surviving the Holocaust: he outsmarted it. He refused to let it steal his humanity. In many ways, his life became a living example of what Dhirubhai Ambani meant by turning adversity into opportunity.

For most of us, adversity does not arrive in the form of war or imprisonment. It arrives quietly, as a loss, a setback, a disappointment, or a dream delayed. Yet the lesson remains the same. We cannot always control what happens to us, but we can choose how we respond.

Reading Eddie's story helped me see that our worst moments can also become the starting point of our best selves. Every struggle carries within it the seed of transformation, if only we are willing to nurture it.

I think of that book often now, not only as a Holocaust story, but as a story of human possibility. It reminds me to be grateful for ordinary things: the comfort of home, the sound of laughter, the ability to call a friend, and the chance to try again.

In today's world, cynicism often seems fashionable and complaining comes easily. In those moments, Eddie Jaku's voice cuts through the noise with a kind of childlike clarity. It reminds us: life will hurt you, but it will also heal you. Do not let one stop you from seeing the other.

The Core Idea

Tomorrow morning, begin your day by writing down one small joy you already have and one challenge you are ready to face again. It will not erase the pain, but it will shift the balance, from what is broken to what is still whole. That is where opportunity begins: not in success, but in the quiet decision to remain kind, hopeful, and deeply human.

42

Trust in Google, but Don't Forget Your Gut

A few years ago, we were driving from Gurgaon to Meerut for a family function. It was one of those bright, sticky afternoons when everyone in the car has an opinion and the driver just wants peace.

As we reached the Ghaziabad border, we came to a confusing crossroad. My wife, ever the voice of reason, said, "Stop and ask someone." I, of course, had more faith in Silicon Valley than in roadside advice. "No need," I said confidently, opening Google Maps. One tap, one blue line. What could possibly go wrong?

Plenty, as it turned out.

The route started out well but quickly turned into a comedy of errors. Google, in its infinite wisdom, decided we needed "the fastest route." Apparently, that meant weaving through tiny villages, broken roads, and narrow lanes where the car barely fit. Every turn brought a new challenge:

potholes deep enough to test our suspension, buffaloes blocking the road, and amused villagers who clearly knew we were lost.

After nearly an hour of this chaos, my wife finally said what I had been trying not to hear. "Maybe we should have just taken the highway."

I stopped to ask a local if there was a way back. He looked at me with the calm pity usually reserved for city drivers and said, "You can go back the way you came, or go forward for another twenty kilometres. Your choice."

My family was not thrilled. The air inside the car grew heavy with muttered complaints and long sighs. But we pressed on, mostly because turning back somehow felt worse than continuing forward.

And then the unexpected happened.

We reached the venue right on time.

Later we discovered that relatives who had taken the highway, the sensible and well-paved route, had been stuck in a massive traffic jam caused by an accident. Google's chaotic detour, frustrating as it had been, had somehow worked in our favour.

On the drive back (this time via the highway, because I was not risking a sequel), I kept thinking about what had just happened.

It was one of those strange days that remind you how life, much like Google Maps, cannot always be followed blindly. And how the shortest route is not necessarily the best one.

Google had data. But I had something else: experience, instinct, and a nervous system that could sense when a road did not feel right.

That day quietly taught me a few lessons about decision-making, the kind no app can make for you.

We live in a time when data seems to have all the answers. Want to invest? There is an algorithm for that. Want to eat healthier? There is an app for that. Want to find your soulmate? There is definitely an app for that too.

But in our eagerness to outsource thinking, we have slowly begun to lose touch with something essential: our own judgement.

Technology can guide us, but it cannot see context. It does not know that a narrow village road may cost you thirty extra minutes of honking, apologising, and reversing to let a tractor pass. It does not know that the passenger in the back seat is losing patience, or that your car's low clearance makes every bump a small gamble.

In life too, our decisions often come down to a quiet tug-of-war between logic and intuition.

Sometimes the numbers make perfect sense, but the gut disagrees. Ignoring that feeling can take us down rough roads.

Yet the opposite is also true.

Sometimes the road that looks messy turns out to be the right one, simply because it avoids a much bigger jam further ahead.

I have seen this happen in business more than once. A project that initially appears off-track becomes the most innovative one. A risky hire turns out to be the most valuable team member. A decision that looks questionable on paper becomes exactly what the situation needed.

Because while data predicts, wisdom interprets.

That is something Google still cannot do. At least, not yet.

Today, I trust technology completely, but I no longer obey it blindly. I use it as a tool, not as a compass. I double-check, ask around, and most importantly, listen to that quiet inner voice that says, "Maybe there is more to this road than the map can see."

My wife, of course, insists she could have told me all this without the detour.

And she is probably right.

The Core Idea

Use every smart tool you can, but never stop thinking for yourself. Tomorrow, when you are about to follow an "expert" suggestion, pause for a moment. Ask yourself whether it truly feels right. Whether it is Google Maps, a consultant's advice, or a trending shortcut, verify, sense, and then decide. Because data may give you the direction, but your instincts reveal the story behind the road. And sometimes, the rough road with buffaloes gets you there faster.

43

The Green Path Behind You

There's a story I once heard from a Guru, one that has stayed with me through many years of professional life.

One morning, the Guru handed his disciple two buckets and asked him to fetch water from a nearby pond. As the young man picked them up, he noticed something unusual. One of the buckets had a small hole in it. By the time he returned from the pond, much of the water had leaked out.

He pointed this out to the Guru, assuming the damaged bucket would be replaced. But the Guru simply smiled and said, "Do as I say."

And so, day after day, the disciple carried the same two buckets along the same path. He tried everything he could think of. He walked faster. He stuffed the hole with cloth. He balanced the bucket more carefully. But nothing worked. No matter what he did, the water kept leaking.

Weeks passed, and frustration slowly began to build inside him. *What is the point of this meaningless task?* he wondered.

One morning, sensing his disciple's unease, the Guru said, "Come, today I will walk with you."

They walked together to the pond and started the journey back. Halfway along the path, the Guru stopped and said, "Look around you, my child. What do you see?"

The disciple looked carefully along the path. One side was dry and dusty. But the other side, the side along which the leaking bucket had always been carried, was lush and green. Flowers, shrubs, and soft grass had grown along the trail.

The Guru smiled gently.

"All this time," he said, "you have been watering the path without even realising it. You thought your effort was being wasted. But it was quietly creating life, just not where you were looking."

That story has stayed with me for years because I have seen its truth play out many times in real life. Projects that seemed to go nowhere for months. People I mentored who didn't appear to change. Ideas that failed at first before eventually succeeding.

Each time, the lesson was the same: effort is rarely wasted. Sometimes its impact simply appears in places we are not immediately watching.

Yet we live in an age that celebrates instant feedback. Success today is often measured through visible signals — likes, shares, views, applause. When those signals do not appear quickly, it is easy to assume that our efforts are going nowhere.

But some of the most meaningful work you will ever do happens quietly, away from the spotlight.

Recently, I read about a woman who deleted her YouTube channel after months of slow growth and very few views. She felt defeated, convinced that nobody cared about what she was creating. In many ways, her story could belong to anyone today. Most of us know what it feels like to put our energy and passion into something and not see it take off.

But what happened next was remarkable.

Her story spread online, and hundreds of people reached out — not to criticise her, but to encourage her. They told her she should not have given up, that her work had value, and that everyone begins slowly.

What struck me most was not her decision to quit, but the response she received. It reminded me that beneath the cynicism we often talk about, there is still a deep respect for persistence. People still admire consistency, quiet effort, and the courage to keep going even when results are small.

In a time when attention spans are shrinking and instant results are glorified, it was heartening to see strangers come together to remind someone — and perhaps themselves — that patience still matters.

We are living in a time when technology changes every day and algorithms shift constantly. Yet one truth has not changed: effort compounds over time.

Whether it is an artist uploading videos online, a teacher guiding students in a classroom, or someone learning AI for the first time at sixty, progress rarely happens overnight. It grows slowly through repetition, discipline, and persistence.

That is why the Guru's story feels more relevant than ever.

Visible effort may not always bring visible results immediately, but it always sets something in motion. It builds discipline, strengthens unseen skills, and prepares you for challenges you have not yet faced.

When you continue working through uncertainty, you are not just moving toward an external goal. You are quietly shaping your inner resilience. And that inner strength often reveals itself later, when you need it most.

I have seen this many times in the workplace. Someone spends years doing steady, unglamorous work — improving systems, mentoring colleagues, solving problems quietly in the background. For a long time, it may seem like nobody notices. But when a real challenge appears, that same person becomes the one everyone depends on.

Suddenly, the value of those unseen efforts becomes clear.

The invisible becomes visible.

The same principle applies to personal growth. Day to day, progress can feel almost invisible. But one day you look back and realise how much you have changed — how much calmer, wiser, and steadier you have become.

That is why the story of the leaking bucket resonates so deeply with me.

Sometimes, when we believe our efforts are leaking away, they are actually nourishing something just outside our field of vision.

And sometimes, the path we are walking is quietly turning green behind us.

The Core Idea

Tomorrow, continue one thing you have been tempted to give up — your side project, your fitness routine, or your attempt to learn something new. Do it quietly, without constantly checking whether it is "working." Then, from time to time, pause and look around. You may discover a patch of green where you least expected it — something growing quietly because of your effort. Because real progress often blooms softly in the background, waiting patiently for you to notice it.

44

Junoon: Be Mad Enough to Succeed

Until Class 4, I studied in a small Hindi-medium school in Kolkata. My world was familiar, my grades among the best, and my confidence unshakable. Then came a sudden leap — admission to St. Lawrence, one of the city's top English-medium schools. Overnight, everything changed. Lessons were in English, and communication in any other language was discouraged. The teachers were kind but firm; the students confident and fluent. I, meanwhile, understood little and spoke even less.

For a twelve-year-old used to excelling, the fall from first to last was more than an academic setback. It felt like humiliation. My confidence crumbled. I dreaded being called upon in class. The boy who once laughed freely now sat quietly at the back, hoping not to be noticed. There was no one to guide me — no coaching classes, no mentor — just the dull ache of failure sitting quietly in my chest.

But one evening, something shifted.

I cannot explain it logically. It wasn't motivation, and it wasn't even hope. It was something simpler and more powerful — anger mixed with resolve. I remember looking at my books and thinking, *I won't let this defeat me.*

That summer, while others played cricket or visited relatives, I made a strange plan. I bought a Cambridge Dictionary, a Wren & Martin grammar book, and a Rapidex English Speaking Course. Then I began what can only be described as madness.

For weeks, I lived with those books. I memorised words, spoke to myself in English, and corrected my own sentences out loud. I would read, repeat, and practice again and again. I studied nearly eighteen hours a day, often falling asleep with the dictionary open beside me.

Looking back now, I do not think it was passion that drove me. Passion is what you feel when you love something. I certainly did not love English grammar.

I simply refused to lose.

What pushed me forward was determination, pure and raw — the kind that grows quietly when you feel you have no other option.

Slowly, things began to change. I started understanding lessons better. The words that once sounded like noise began to make sense. I found myself raising my hand again in class. By the next year, the boy who had once been mocked for his poor English was among the better students.

But more important than the marks was a deeper discovery. I realised that I could rebuild myself from scratch.

That summer taught me that willpower is not something you are born with. It is something you build, moment by moment, every time you decide not to stop.

Determination even has a strange biology behind it. Scientists say it is not just mental; it is chemical as well. When you push past pain or exhaustion, your brain releases dopamine — the so-called "reward" chemical. It is the same chemical that rises when you accomplish a goal, or even take a meaningful step toward one.

Each small win, each moment of perseverance, quietly trains your brain to believe: *I can do this.*

That is why determination feeds on itself. The more you push forward, the stronger you become.

History and everyday life are full of such examples.

Take mountaineer Arunima Sinha, who lost a leg after being thrown off a moving train and still became the first female amputee to climb Mount Everest. Or Thomas Edison, who famously said he did not fail a thousand times — he simply found a thousand ways that did not work. Or Mary Kom, who kept fighting — literally — through social ridicule, motherhood, and financial hardship to become a world champion.

None of them began because they loved pain or struggle. They simply refused to give up.

Determination, I have realised, is rarely loud. It does not look glamorous or exciting the way passion sometimes does. It is quiet, repetitive, and often boring. It shows up long after the excitement has faded.

It is the reason runners finish marathons long after the thrill of the starting line disappears. It is what keeps soldiers marching, entrepreneurs trying again after failure, patients fighting illness, and students returning to their books.

That is what *junoon* really is — not the excitement of a spark, but the endurance of a flame.

There is another lesson that experience taught me.

When you see someone struggling, do not laugh and do not look away. Support the "Rajneesh" in your life — the one trying, failing, and trying again.

Even a small word of encouragement can make a difference.

During my lowest phase, a classmate once told me quietly, "Don't worry, you'll get there." Just that — nothing dramatic. Yet I remember it to this day. Sometimes belief travels faster when someone else carries it for you.

That struggle also deepened my respect for my mother tongue.

Ironically, the harder I worked to learn English, the more I appreciated Hindi. Language, I realised, is not a measure of intelligence; it is an expression of culture. Fluency does not define a person's worth. Confidence does.

Over the years, I have seen the same pattern repeat — in work, in relationships, and in every difficult season of life. You do not overcome challenges with talent or luck alone.

You overcome them with a decision.

A stubborn, everyday decision to keep moving.

When people say "follow your passion," I nod politely. But experience has taught me that passion alone rarely builds anything lasting. Passion may start the journey, but it is discipline that keeps you walking when the road becomes hard.

Passion makes you begin.

Determination makes you finish.

That summer taught me far more than English. It taught me self-respect. It taught me that failure is never permanent — but giving up can be.

The next time you face a wall, remember this: the wall is not there to stop you.

It is there to test how badly you want to cross it.

The Core Idea

Think of something that once set you back — a subject that defeated you, a skill that made you feel small, or a challenge you quietly walked away from. Tomorrow, take one small step towards it. Open the book again. Make the call. Try once more. Now imagine what it would feel like to master it. To return to that same battlefield and walk away victorious this time. The pride. The calm. The quiet satisfaction of knowing that you did not stop.

45

The Weight of Doubt

A few years ago, a close friend of mine suddenly went silent.

No calls. No replies to messages. Nothing.

We had worked together for years, shared hundreds of cups of tea, travelled together. Then one day, it felt as if he had simply walked out of the friendship.

At first, I brushed it off. "He's probably busy," I told myself. But as the weeks went by, that silence began to sting.

Did I say something wrong? Did I let him down somehow?

I replayed our conversations in my head, trying to spot what might have gone wrong. The more I thought about it, the more stories I built in my mind. Every unanswered message started to feel personal.

Eventually, I stopped calling him altogether.

Months later, out of the blue, I received a short message.

"Sorry I disappeared. I wasn't keeping well. Needed time to get better before talking to anyone."

That one message hit me harder than I expected.

He hadn't forgotten me. He hadn't been angry. He was simply unwell — struggling quietly, and I had assumed the worst.

I felt both relieved and a little ashamed.

Because that's what doubt does. It fills silence with noise. It turns pauses into problems.

If I had just picked up the phone and asked once, instead of analysing everything in my head, I could have saved months of unnecessary distance. That experience taught me something simple but powerful: when in doubt, ask — don't assume.

Yet we live in a time when doubt has almost become second nature.

Parents worry, "Will my children care for me when I'm old?"

Children wonder, "Do my parents love my sibling more?"

Students suspect teachers of favouritism. Teachers suspect their principals.

Employees think the boss promotes only the "yes-men." Bosses think their teams aren't being honest.

Even at home, it's the same. A wife suspects her husband; he suspects her. The mother-in-law and daughter-in-law story? The script hasn't changed in centuries.

And when it comes to faith, we even begin doubting God. "Are my prayers no longer being heard?"

Slowly, almost without noticing, we begin to question everything.

We call it being practical or cautious. But truthfully, it's exhausting.

Doubt doesn't arrive like a storm. It seeps in like damp — slowly, silently — until one day everything feels a little weaker.

And what's worse, it isolates us.

Doubt builds invisible walls — between colleagues, between family members, between friends — and sometimes even between us and ourselves.

There's a line I once came across that explains it beautifully:

We judge others by their actions, but ourselves by our intentions.

Think about that for a moment.

When we make a mistake, we know we didn't mean harm — so we excuse ourselves. But when someone else makes a mistake, we judge the action, not the intention. That is where doubt quietly takes root. We hold others to a harsher standard than we hold ourselves.

If we could just flip that — if we could begin judging others by their intentions, and ourselves by our actions — half our conflicts would disappear overnight.

Trust begins right there.

In giving others the same benefit of doubt that we so easily give ourselves.

It reminds me of Yudhishthira from the Mahabharata — the man everyone called Dharmaraj, the pillar of truth. He was respected for his honesty, but even he was not free from doubt.

When Duryodhana invited him to play the game of dice, everyone warned him — his brothers, Draupadi, even Vidura. They could see the danger clearly. But Yudhishthira hesitated to trust them. He believed they were being emotional, that he understood the situation better.

In that moment, he trusted the game more than the people who loved him.

And that mistake cost him everything — his kingdom, his freedom, and his peace.

During exile, when he finally had time to reflect, Yudhishthira realised that his greatest failure wasn't losing the game — it was losing faith. He had doubted the intentions of those who truly cared for him. And once that trust was shaken, everything else followed.

That's the strange thing about doubt. In the moment, it feels clever, cautious, even wise. But very often it ends up breaking things that are not easy to rebuild.

I have seen this in teams as well. The most successful teams are not always the ones with the brightest individuals. They are the ones where people trust each other. Where someone can say, "I made a mistake," and the rest respond, "Alright, let's fix it." Where credit is shared freely, and no one is constantly watching their back because everyone knows they are supported.

Trust builds speed. Doubt slows everything down.

The same is true in families. When trust lives in a home, life flows easily. Even silence feels comfortable. But when doubt enters, it quietly fills every corner. Every word begins to sound like an accusation. Every action invites suspicion. And before long, love turns into a tally sheet.

Of course, I'm not suggesting that we trust blindly. Life does bring its share of betrayals and disappointments. But if you spend your entire life waiting for guarantees, you will never truly connect with anyone.

Forgiveness heals faster than suspicion ever can.

It takes courage to trust. And it takes even more courage to trust again after being hurt. But that is the only way to live freely.

Because trust is not about being naïve. It is about choosing peace over constant paranoia. It is saying, "Even if

I get hurt once in a while, I would rather live with an open heart than a guarded one."

Every meaningful thing in this world stands on trust — love, friendship, teamwork, faith.

Without it, everything slowly collapses under its own weight.

So perhaps, in this age of second-guessing and constant suspicion, we can try something simpler:

Trust a little more.

Trust your child to make mistakes and learn.

Trust your colleague to mean well.

Trust your partner's silence.

Trust that life, somehow, has your back.

And if you pray — trust that someone, somewhere, is listening.

Because in the end, life rarely rewards suspicion. It rewards faith.

The Core Idea

Tomorrow morning, call a friend you haven't spoken to in a while. Or clear a doubt that has been sitting quietly in your heart. Don't overthink it — just reach out. You may be surprised how often love and trust are waiting on the other end, wondering why you didn't call sooner. Because sometimes, rebuilding trust takes nothing more than a single honest conversation.

PART 8

Time, Love & What Truly Remains

46

Before the World Wakes Up

I belong to the 5 a.m. club.

Not because I read about it somewhere or followed a trend. It's simply something that has been part of my life for years.

One reason for whatever little success I've had is the habit of getting up early. I have a particular routine: I go for a walk before sunrise because I always want to see the rising sun.

That moment — when the first streak of light appears on the horizon — does something to me. I believe, and many people who experience it would agree, that watching the rising sun puts you in what I call a spiritual blank state.

It's difficult to describe unless you've felt it.

The world is quiet. The air is cool. And for a few seconds, your mind becomes completely still. You're not thinking about the day ahead, not checking your phone, not planning or worrying. You're simply standing there — blank, but in a good way.

And in that blankness, something interesting often happens.

If I think about something that has been troubling me — a work problem, a personal issue, something I cannot seem to solve — suddenly an answer flashes through my mind. It may just be my faith speaking, but almost every time that flash turns out to be right. I've followed those instincts again and again, and most of the time they have worked.

It almost feels as if the rising sun carries a message meant just for that moment — if you are awake and quiet enough to receive it.

The other thing it does is fill you with energy. Even people who are not spiritual will agree that watching the sunrise creates a certain surge inside you. A kind of quiet power. It's not about exercise or discipline. It's simply the energy that comes from seeing a new day being born right in front of you.

It changes your mood completely.

When your mind isn't crowded with noise, you think calmly and make better decisions. Instead of reacting immediately, you allow ideas to settle and take shape.

Being an early riser has also helped me in practical ways. From the beginning of my career, I developed the habit of reaching the office before everyone else. Even arriving half an hour early can change the entire rhythm of your day.

By the time others walk in, you've already cleared your emails, given instructions, and planned your priorities. You are relaxed.

They are the ones feeling pressure. You are the one in control.

That one simple habit — starting the day before others — gives you a quiet edge. You are not competing with anyone. You are simply ahead.

And it's not only about efficiency. That calm head start gives you time to think — not just act. You have the space to look at the bigger picture, notice details others might miss, and stay one step ahead without rushing.

Over the years, I've realised that many of my good decisions — both personal and professional — were made either during or right after my early morning walks. Something about that hour clears the fog in your mind. You begin to see things more clearly.

People often ask how I manage to wake up so early every single day.

I don't follow any complicated system. I simply sleep before midnight so I can get about five hours of deep sleep. More importantly, I genuinely look forward to those few quiet minutes before the world wakes up. It feels like a small appointment I have with myself.

And it's one I don't like to miss.

Whenever I skip it — during travel or after late nights — I feel the difference almost immediately. The day feels heavier. My thoughts aren't as sharp. I become more reactive. It's almost like missing your daily dose of clarity.

So yes, I belong to the 5 a.m. club — my own version of it.

No slogans.

No strict rules.

No fancy routine.

Just a walk, a rising sun, and a few quiet moments that somehow manage to put everything else in place.

If you're struggling with something right now — big or small — try this once. Go out before sunrise. Don't think, don't plan, just watch. And when the sun appears, ask your question silently.

You might be surprised at the answer that flashes back at you.

The Core Idea

Tomorrow, wake up just twenty minutes earlier than usual. Step outside before sunrise, leave your phone behind, and do nothing except watch the light arrive. Don't plan. Don't analyse. Just be still. Clarity often shows up when the world is quiet enough for you to hear it.

47

When You Believe, Things Move

Before every exam, my mother would give me a spoonful of *dahi-cheeni*. It was her way of saying, "Have faith. You'll do well."

I always did — and strangely, it almost always worked.

I think that's where my understanding of faith began. The act of praying before an exam, touching your parents' feet, or simply closing your eyes for a moment before an important meeting — these small rituals shift something inside you. You leave your tension behind and hand it over to something larger than yourself.

Whether God actually intervenes or not depends on one's faith, but what truly changes in that moment is *you*. You shed your nervousness. You stop doubting yourself. You feel lighter, calmer, more in control.

That's faith — the quiet bridge between fear and confidence.

I have seen this play out many times in my life, but one moment stands out clearly.

A few years ago, I travelled to the Amarnath Temple. My wife didn't join me — she prefers slower, more relaxed trips. So two of my colleagues accompanied me. We flew to Srinagar and then drove to Pahalgam, from where we planned to take a helicopter the next morning to reach close to the shrine.

Anyone who has done the Amarnath Yatra knows how unpredictable it can be. There are long treks, sudden weather changes, and thousands of pilgrims hoping for a smooth *darshan*. Usually, I make sure everything is well organised — passes, permissions, helicopter timing — because the travel window is often very tight.

This time, I had asked one of my colleagues to handle the arrangements. He assured me everything was done. But when we reached and checked, we realised the arrangements were incomplete. The coordination at the shrine end had not been handled properly.

Naturally, I was upset. I like precision in everything.

I made a few quick calls and fixed what I could. Just as I began to feel settled again, the weather suddenly turned. Dark clouds gathered, and soon it began raining heavily — the kind of mountain rain that stops everything. Helicopters stop flying, and your entire plan collapses.

That night, the rain kept pouring.

My colleagues suggested we cancel the trip and head back. But something inside me said, *Wait.*

I have always believed that when you go on a spiritual journey, it is not you who decides the timing — it is God. If He wants you to come, you will. If He doesn't, no amount of planning will help.

So I told them, "Let's not worry. If it's meant to happen, it will. If not, that's fine too."

We had dinner and went to sleep.

At dawn, as always, I woke up early. Around 5:30, I walked to the window and drew back the curtains.

Bright sunlight poured in.

Not a single cloud was in sight. The same valley that had been drenched and dark just a few hours earlier was now sparkling clean — washed by the rain and glowing in golden light.

I called my colleagues. They couldn't believe it.

The weather was perfect. The helicopter was ready. And we completed the Amarnath Yatra exactly as planned.

That, to me, is the power of faith.

But does having faith mean you sit idle and wait for miracles?

Absolutely not.

Faith means doing your best and then trusting the process. It means letting go of anxiety once you have done what you can.

Many bestselling books describe this idea in different ways. *The Secret*, for instance, calls it the Law of Attraction — the idea that what you believe deeply begins to shape your reality. Napoleon Hill, in *Think and Grow Rich*, wrote that "faith is the head chemist of the mind."

Even before I read those books, I understood one thing instinctively: when you have faith, you stop resisting. You move from fear into flow.

I'm sure you have experienced moments like this in your own life.

Sometimes the results may come from your hard work rather than faith alone. But before the results arrive, faith keeps you reassured and hopeful — and that itself is powerful.

A friend of mine recently shared a story about his daughter. She had a panic attack the night before her board exam results were announced. The whole family sat together, folded their hands, and prayed quietly for a few minutes.

When they opened their eyes, the mother said softly, "I have a very good feeling about this."

Those few moments of calm and optimism helped relax the daughter. The next morning they received wonderful news — she had topped the board.

Faith may not be the main driver of success, but it certainly gives you the confidence to shift into the right gears.

Most of us live somewhere between belief and doubt. We say we have faith, but we continue worrying at the same time. It is like holding the steering wheel and the handbrake together. And that is why we feel stuck.

True faith, in my view, is not 99 percent. It is 100 percent.

Either you believe, or you don't.

That night in Pahalgam, when I chose not to worry, I could easily have spent hours pacing the room, calling people, checking weather forecasts. Instead, I trusted the process and slept peacefully.

That peace itself changed something — maybe not the weather, but certainly my state of mind.

And when your state of mind changes, the world often begins to cooperate in unexpected ways.

So the next time you face uncertainty, remember this: believe fully, act wisely, and then let go.

Things may not always go exactly the way you planned. But more often than not — when you truly believe — things begin to move.

The Core Idea

When in doubt, close your eyes for a minute, take a deep breath, and let go. Faith begins where effort ends — and calm often moves things faster than anxiety ever can.

48

The Hand on the Shoulder

I once heard a beautiful story from Arya Samaj Pandit Bheem Sen Shastriji.

It is simple, but it has stayed with me — perhaps because it says something profound about how we draw strength in life.

A father once walked up to his grown-up son, placed his hand on his shoulder, and asked, "Tell me, who do you think is stronger between the two of us?"

The son, without hesitation, replied, "Of course I am, Dad."

The father stepped back, a little surprised. He thought to himself, *Has my son become so proud that he thinks he's stronger than me?*

He walked away quietly, but after a moment he turned back. This time he asked the same question again.

"Who is stronger, you or me?"

The son smiled and replied, "No, Father — it's you who's stronger."

Now the father was completely puzzled.

"Just a minute ago," he said, "you told me you were stronger. How can both be true?"

The son looked at him warmly and said, "Dad, the first time you asked, your hand was on my shoulder. When your hand is there, I feel I can take on the whole world. But when you moved away, I realised — without you beside me, how could I possibly be stronger than you?"

That story carries a lot of truth.

We often think strength means independence — standing tall on our own, proving that we don't need anyone's help. But real strength, as the son reminds us, often comes from the invisible hands that support us — parents, mentors, friends, colleagues, and sometimes even complete strangers who believe in us when we don't yet believe in ourselves.

When I look back at my own life, I see the same pattern.

Every time I have managed to do something difficult, there has always been a guiding hand somewhere — a word of encouragement, a quiet blessing, or simply someone's belief that I could handle it.

I think of my father, who never lectured but always led by example. Or of a teacher who once told me, "Don't rush to prove yourself — you'll have a lifetime for that." At the time, it sounded like a simple remark. Today, I realise how much wisdom was packed into those few words.

We often underestimate how powerful these small gestures are — a hand on the shoulder, a reassuring smile, a quiet "you'll be fine." Yet those simple moments can carry someone through an entire storm.

This same idea appears in many books that have inspired millions. In *The Monk Who Sold His Ferrari*, Robin Sharma talks about how every meaningful achievement begins with inner faith — a strength often sparked by mentors and guides. In *The Alchemist*, Santiago finds his "personal legend" only because he listens to the quiet guidance around him — from the old king, from the desert, and from the universe that keeps nudging him forward.

That is the "hand on the shoulder."

You cannot always see it, but it is there — guiding, protecting, and reminding you that you are not alone in your climb.

Even in our own lives, we have protectors — sometimes human, sometimes divine.

I remember when I started my career. There were days when I felt uncertain and unsure of myself. But I also remember the quiet confidence my father had in me. He never lectured, never pushed advice forcefully, but I could feel his hand on my shoulder — in every word of encouragement, in every calm "Don't worry, you'll figure it out."

That kind of faith slowly becomes part of you. It shapes the way you face life.

I think that is what the story truly teaches us: the hand of the protector makes you fearless. When you know someone believes in you, you stop doubting yourself. You take risks. You fail, stand up again, and keep moving forward.

Maybe that is why so many of us still whisper a prayer before an important moment — an exam, an interview, a journey, or the beginning of a new chapter in life. It is our way of feeling that hand on the shoulder again.

It is faith — human or divine — that gives us the courage to move forward.

So whenever you feel overwhelmed, pause for a moment and remember that story. Ask yourself: whose hand is on my shoulder? Who has quietly given me strength along the way?

And if you can, be that hand for someone else.

Because the moment your hand rests on another person's shoulder, you are not just offering support — you are reminding them of their own strength.

That, to me, is the true meaning of the protector's hand.

The Core Idea

Once a week, tell someone exactly what you trust them with or believe in them for. Not advice. Not correction. Just belief. Often, that single gesture becomes the hand on the shoulder that carries someone through difficult terrain.

49

Call Me When Free…

I once knew a young man who had a small argument with his father over the phone. He hung up abruptly, thinking he would apologise later. That night, his father suffered a heart attack and never woke up.

For months, the son couldn't sleep. Every time he picked up his phone, he saw his father's last message: *Call me when free.* That single line haunted him.

He once told me quietly, "I would give everything I have for one more chance to call him back."

That's the thing about time — it doesn't always give you second chances.

On the same theme, I once heard a story from Pandit Bheem Sen Shastriji, and it has stayed with me ever since.

A grown-up son, flushed with success, goes to his mother one day and says, "Dear mother, you have done so much for me. I want to repay your kindness. Please ask for anything — gold, a house, money — whatever you desire."

His mother smiles gently and says, "Dear son, I only wish for your companionship, nothing more."

But the son insists. "No, Mother, please tell me what you truly want."

After a moment, she says, "All right. Can you sleep beside me tonight?"

The son laughs, relieved. "Is that all? Of course, Mother, I'll sleep beside you."

Later that night, about an hour after they lie down, the mother wakes her son.

"I'm thirsty. Can you please get me some water?"

The son, half asleep, gets up, pours a glass of water, and hands it to her. She takes a few sips and then accidentally spills the rest on the bed.

Patiently, he cleans it up and lies down again.

An hour later, it happens again. And then again.

After the third time, he finally loses his temper.

"Mother," he says, "why do you keep spilling the water? How do you expect me to sleep on this wet bed?"

The mother looks at him gently and says, "My dear son, you cannot bear to sleep on a wet bed for one night. But when you were a child, you wet the bed almost every hour. I would quietly shift you from one side to another, trying to find a dry spot for you — and I slept on the wet side."

The son is struck silent. He takes her hand and weeps.

That story never fails to move me. It is simple, but it carries the entire weight of what love really means — quiet sacrifice, invisible effort, and an affection that asks for nothing in return.

No matter how much we achieve or how far we travel, there is no currency on earth that can repay a mother's care. When you think about it, love like that almost feels beyond this world. It is unconditional, tireless, and endlessly forgiving.

In the *Ramayana*, when Kaikeyi demanded that Lord Rama go into exile, his mother Kausalya did not stop him, even though her heart must have been breaking. She did not hold him back or curse fate. She simply blessed him, knowing that sometimes love means letting go, even when it tears you apart.

That is the quiet strength of a mother — to place her child's path above her own peace.

And yet, somewhere along the way, we forget.

We begin treating love like something to schedule — a quick call, a brief message on Mother's Day, a gift ordered online. But what our parents truly crave is not the gift; it is the thought. Not the money, but the moment.

In *Tuesdays with Morrie*, Mitch Albom writes, "There is no such thing as 'too late' in life, but there is such a thing as 'too long.'"

Too long to say sorry.

Too long to say thank you.

Too long to say *I love you.*

And yet, it is never too late to begin now.

Call your parents. Sit with them. Ask them about their stories. They have lived through more than we can imagine, and their wisdom comes from battles quietly fought, nights spent awake, and tears wiped away before anyone noticed.

Even if they have passed on, the love they gave you does not end there. The best way to honour it is to pass it forward

— to care for someone who needs a guiding hand, to offer comfort without being asked, and to live with the same quiet grace they once showed you.

Perhaps that is how we keep them alive — not through grand tributes or emotional posts, but through the way we live each day.

In the end, love like a mother's cannot really be repaid. It can only be remembered — and continued.

Because when everything else fades, what remains is that invisible hand that once rested on your head, that sleepless night someone spent beside you, and that unwavering belief that you would grow into someone good.

There is an old saying: *Because God couldn't be everywhere, He made mothers.*

Few lines capture the truth of love more simply than that.

The Core Idea

Fix one non-negotiable connection ritual. Decide today: a weekly call, a daily good-night message, or a monthly meal together — and put it on your calendar. Treat it like an appointment you never cancel.

50

Why I Run a Little Faster

Some people chase success.

I've always chased time.

It's not that I'm in a hurry — I simply prefer to arrive before the world wakes up. To have that quiet stretch of clarity before the noise begins. For me, staying ahead has always meant preparing for life before it happens.

I don't remember anyone teaching me this habit. In fact, most people in my joint family of twenty-five were rather relaxed about things. But I was always a bit of an oddity.

We used to get only one newspaper. If you didn't grab it first, you had to wait until it was a crumpled, chai-stained relic by noon. So I began waking up at five, tiptoeing to the door to catch the paper while everyone else slept. I loved the crisp, fresh feel of the pages in my hands. Reading the headlines before anyone else gave me a secret thrill.

At breakfast, my cousins teased me for always choosing to sit in the hot kitchen for meals. But I had my reason — I wanted my chapati straight off the griddle, still puffed and steaming. My logic was simple: why wait for it to go cold when you can enjoy it hot?

At school, I was always the first one ready. Bag packed, shoes polished, homework done. My friends found it amusing that I would rather arrive early and wait alone at the gate than rush and risk being late.

That small discipline became a habit — almost a muscle — one that I still rely on today.

Even later, in my first job, I would reach the office before everyone else. Those first thirty minutes of stillness — no emails, no meetings — became sacred. They helped me plan the day, anticipate obstacles, and glide through what others stumbled over.

Even now, I sometimes use digital tools early in the morning to get approvals or decisions moving before the day officially begins. It isn't cleverness. It's simply rhythm.

But here is something I learnt later — staying ahead doesn't mean pulling everyone else along at your speed.

A friend of mine discovered this the hard way. He was the kind of person who ran his home like a perfectly oiled machine. Breakfast at eight. School drop-off at exactly eight-thirty. Lights out at ten. His wife often joked that even their laughter had to be scheduled.

One evening at dinner, he was fussing because the rotis weren't ready "on time." The children had wandered off, and the television was playing in the background. His wife quietly put down her spoon, looked at him, and said, "You know, for years I've lived by your clock. But today I realised something — I want to live life at my own pace."

It wasn't an argument. It was a moment of truth.

She wasn't asking for rebellion. She was simply asking for room to breathe.

And my friend, who had spent years ensuring that everything ran efficiently, suddenly understood that not everyone finds peace in precision. Some people find it in pauses.

It reminded me of *Eat, Pray, Love* — Elizabeth Gilbert's story of leaving behind a life that was stable and structured but starved of spontaneity. She wasn't escaping responsibility; she was reclaiming rhythm. Sometimes, you need to slow down to rediscover your natural pace.

Since then, I've tried to live with that balance.

I still wake up early, plan my day, and reach meetings before time. But I have learnt not to turn my pace into pressure for others. I avoid sending late-night messages to colleagues, and I don't hover around family members when they are running late.

Discipline, I've realised, is personal. It should never become a burden for someone else.

These small rituals keep me grounded:

A morning walk timed with sunrise — nature's quiet reminder that every day begins slowly and steadily.

A few silent minutes before bed to review the day — not to criticise myself, but simply to reflect.

And on Sundays, I plan my week just enough to stay steady, not stressed.

I'm not sending out a mixed message here.

I'm simply saying — make haste slowly.

Stay prepared, but not pressured.

Stay ahead, but not at the cost of peace.

Run a little faster if you want to stay ahead of the race — just make sure your heart has time to catch up.

The Core Idea

Create a daily head start that belongs only to you — even twenty quiet minutes before the day takes over. Use it to think, not react. To prepare, not rush. Stay disciplined about your own pace, but do not impose it on others. Real advantage comes from starting early — and living gently.

51

The River That Never Runs Dry

Every year, when the monsoon plays truant, Mumbai reminds you what scarcity feels like.

The taps run dry, the lakes sink a little lower, and suddenly water — the one thing you once took for granted — becomes precious.

A few years ago, our residential society began water rationing: two hours, twice a day. Naturally, everyone panicked. One resident suggested something surprising.

"What if we keep the supply constant instead of cutting it off? Maybe people will use less."

It sounded odd at first, but he wasn't entirely wrong.

The moment scarcity appears, human instinct kicks in — we begin to hoard. People in our building installed extra tanks, filled them to the brim "just in case," and ironically ended up consuming more water than before.

That's when I realised something important: the fear of losing something often creates the very loss we are trying to avoid.

And this is true not just for water or money — but for knowledge as well.

In offices, classrooms, even within families, I've often seen people hold back what they know. They guard their information like treasure, afraid that if they share it, someone else might catch up — or worse, get ahead. I've seen managers who never properly trained their juniors because they wanted to remain indispensable. I've seen colleagues hold on to ideas until the "perfect" moment to reveal them.

But here is the truth I learnt, both the hard way and the happy way.

Knowledge behaves very much like water.

When it is allowed to flow, it stays fresh. When you hoard it, it begins to stagnate.

Years ago, a young colleague joined my team straight out of college. He was curious but slow to grasp things at first. Initially, I found it easier to simply complete tasks myself rather than spend time explaining them.

But one day, I decided to walk him through a client proposal step by step. It took longer than I expected, but something interesting happened.

As I began explaining the process, I realised that some of my own methods were outdated. There were habits I had carried for years simply because they had once worked.

Mehul's questions — innocent and sometimes blunt — forced me to think more carefully about why I did things a certain way.

In the process of teaching him, I ended up learning more about my own work.

Within a few months, Mehul was no longer struggling. In fact, he started bringing fresh ideas to the table. Today, he runs his own firm — and every time we meet, he still thanks me for that one session.

What I rarely tell him is that I probably learnt more from that hour than he did.

That is the real magic of sharing what you know. It sharpens you. It humbles you. And most importantly, it keeps you relevant.

Because knowledge is not a currency meant to be stored away. It is a current that needs to move.

India has understood this idea for centuries. The *Guru–Shishya Parampara* was never just about hierarchy. It was about continuity — passing light from one lamp to another.

And when the lamp beside you burns brighter, your own flame does not grow dimmer. It simply spreads more warmth.

Yet in today's world of personal branding and competition, we often behave as if every idea is intellectual property and every insight a competitive advantage.

But wisdom does not work that way.

You cannot lock it inside a vault. It has to breathe, circulate, and be shared. That is when it multiplies.

I have noticed this pattern in the leaders I admire most. The truly successful ones are generous with their time and experience. They share their failures openly. They give credit freely.

Because they understand a simple truth: when others grow, the entire ecosystem grows with them.

It is very similar to our water story.

When our society allowed water to flow freely instead of restricting it, people naturally began to use less. Abundance created balance. Scarcity had created panic.

The same principle applies to knowledge.

So the next time you feel the urge to hold back — an idea, a lesson you've learnt, or a contact who could help someone — pause for a moment.

You are not protecting your advantage. You may actually be shrinking it.

Every time you teach someone, you reinforce what you know. Every time you share, you build trust.

And trust, like flowing water, always finds its way back to you.

So share your insights. Mentor that intern. Guide the new entrepreneur. Help the colleague struggling with something you already understand.

You are not giving away your strength.

You are multiplying it.

Because in truth, knowledge follows the same law as kindness:

The more you give, the wiser — and richer — you become.

The Core Idea

This week, deliberately share one thing you would normally hold back — a process you have perfected, a lesson learnt from a mistake, or a useful contact. Do it without expecting credit or return. Then notice what happens: clarity in your own thinking, deeper trust in your relationships, and a quiet strengthening of your relevance. Like water, knowledge stays alive only when it flows.

52

The Things Worth Bringing Back

A few years ago, I began making small changes at home. Nothing dramatic — just little shifts that seemed to make sense.

I stopped buying bottled water and went back to using steel flasks. I switched from chemical cleaners to simple lemon-and-vinegar solutions. I even began making my own toothpaste — a mix of neem, clove, and a pinch of salt, much like my grandmother used to. In the kitchen, we replaced plastic scrubbing pads with ones made from coconut coir.

At first, it was just curiosity — an experiment to see whether the "old ways" still worked.

But somewhere along the way, it began to feel right.

Things lasted longer. Waste reduced naturally. Life, in a quiet way, slowed down to a more comfortable rhythm.

I am sure you must have noticed this too: our grandparents were wiser than we often give them credit for. When they said, "*Jo mil jaaye, uski izzat karo*" — respect what you have — they meant everything: food, time, people, even rainwater.

Of course, they lived with fewer resources and fewer conveniences. Yet there is a quiet irony today — in the name of sustainability and minimalism, we are slowly rediscovering the same habits they lived by every day.

And that, in many ways, is a good thing.

When I look around now, I see how modern life has come full circle. Clay bottles are back in stores. People are rediscovering the joy of hand-ground spices, handmade soaps, and unpolished rice. Even cow dung cakes — once associated only with village kitchens — are now sold online as "natural fuel."

We are not really inventing anything new.

We are remembering.

Even at work, I notice the same shift in thinking. Processes are being redesigned to reuse, recycle, and simplify. Somewhere, instinctively, we seem to be returning to balance.

We are realising that progress does not have to mean excess.

And what we forget, Mother Earth eventually reminds us.

A few months ago, during a visit to my ancestral village, I noticed something small but meaningful. A group of women were drying grain in the courtyard. As the wind picked up, one of them covered the baskets with old cotton cloths instead of plastic sheets

When I asked why, she smiled and said, "*Kapda saans leta hai, plastic ghutan deta hai.*"

Cloth breathes. Plastic suffocates.

Simple. Poetic. And truer than many scientific reports.

That is the beauty of traditional wisdom. It worked because it came from observation, intuition, and a deep connection with nature.

Our ancestors may not have had degrees in design or ecology, but they understood something we often forget today — how closely our lives are tied to the rhythms of the natural world.

Losing that connection is what has brought us to many of the problems we now face.

Sometimes I think modern life is like a suitcase we keep overpacking. Every few years, it becomes too heavy to lift. When we finally open it, we realise that half the things inside were never really necessary.

Maybe it is time to unpack a little.

The Core Idea

Use less plastic. Waste less food. Repair things before replacing them. Walk more. Talk more. Sit in the sunlight for ten minutes instead of scrolling through it on a screen. I am not trying to romanticise the past or speak from nostalgia alone. These are simply practices that worked — and may still help heal the way we live today. One final thought on this thread: let us borrow what still makes sense. Because perhaps progress is not about leaving everything behind. Perhaps it is about knowing what is worth bringing along.

PART 9

My Top 10 Rules for Professionals

Over the years, I've realised that a successful professional life is not built through one grand achievement, but through hundreds of small habits practised quietly, consistently, and often without applause. These aren't theories borrowed from a management book; they are lessons I have lived, observed, and shared with every young colleague who has ever asked me, "Sir, what really helps someone grow?"

So here are my ten simple rules — or perhaps better described as gentle reminders — that can shape your career far more than any degree or title ever will.

1. Knowledge is your greatest asset. Never miss an opportunity to learn.

If there is one thing no one can take away from you, it is what you carry inside your mind. Industries evolve, tools become obsolete, and trends come and go — but knowledge stays with you.

I still meet young professionals who say, "Sir, I'll learn when I need it." The truth is that by the time you "need it," the opportunity may already have passed. Learn proactively. Pick up a book, enrol in a course, or simply have a meaningful conversation. You never know when a single line of insight will change the entire trajectory of your work.

2. No job is trivial or unimportant.

I began my career doing tasks that no one else wanted to handle — filing papers, coordinating follow-ups, organising documents. Yet those small responsibilities taught me clarity, discipline, and humility. These skills proved far more valuable in the long run than any glamorous assignment.

Whatever comes to your table, approach it with sincerity. Success rarely begins with a "big role"; it begins with the seriousness you bring to the smallest responsibility.

3. End your day knowing you added value.

When you leave the office each evening, ask yourself a simple question: *Did I justify my chair today?*

This is not meant to create pressure. Even improving one document, making one thoughtful decision, or handling one call better than expected counts as value. If the honest answer is "not today," that awareness itself is the first step toward doing better tomorrow.

4. Set stiff deadlines for yourself — and then surprise yourself.

Work has a strange tendency to expand and fill the time we give it. If you truly want to stand out, shorten that time. Push your own limits. Challenge your pace.

The thrill of beating your own deadline is addictive. More importantly, it builds trust. People begin to rely on you because they know you deliver earlier than promised. That reputation alone can open doors you never imagined.

5. Never fear a new challenge. That's what separates excellence from mediocrity.

Early in my career, I once said "yes" to a role for which I had absolutely no prior experience. I was nervous — perhaps even a little terrified. But that discomfort became my greatest teacher.

Challenges stretch your abilities, introduce you to new skills, and reveal strengths you did not even know you possessed. If something scares you slightly, it may be exactly the opportunity you should accept. Growth rarely hides inside comfort zones.

6. Be a finisher.

Many people begin with enthusiasm. Few develop the discipline to finish.

I have met professionals who start twenty projects and complete none. And I have met others who start two tasks and complete both with excellence. Guess which ones rise faster?

The world remembers outcomes, not just intentions. Develop the habit of finishing what you begin. That single discipline will take you further than you think.

7. Develop an eye for detail.

The larger the organisation, the higher the stakes. A small oversight can cost crores, reputations, or relationships.

Read documents twice. Verify numbers carefully. Revisit the brief before finalising your work. Attention to detail protects you and strengthens your credibility. It makes your work dependable.

8. Honour time and discipline.

There is something deeply powerful about a person who respects time — both their own and others'.

Reach the office on time. Join meetings punctually. Complete tasks when promised. Even small habits like respecting lunch breaks reflect how you manage yourself.

Discipline builds reliability. And when people know you are dependable, they naturally involve you in larger and more important decisions.

9. Remember: Individual brilliance wins battles. Teamwork wins wars.

You may be the smartest person in the room, but without collective effort, progress will always remain limited.

Help colleagues when they struggle. Share credit generously. Step in when needed. A team built on trust can achieve far more than a room full of individuals competing with one another.

If you want to grow quickly, collaborate.

If you want to grow sustainably, uplift others.

10. Make winning a habit — but don't obsess over the outcome.

Give your full effort to the process. Respect your work. Strive for excellence in whatever you do.

But do not allow outcomes — promotions, awards, recognition — to define your identity. They will arrive when they are meant to.

What stays with you forever is the quiet satisfaction of knowing you gave your best.

Winning is wonderful.

But a calm, guilt-free conscience is even better.

These ten rules are not shortcuts to success. They are a foundation.

If you follow even half of them sincerely, you will notice a shift — in how people perceive you, in how opportunities come your way, and in how confidently you walk your own path.

Because the truth is simple: a professional is not built by chance.

A professional is built by habits — daily, consistent, intentional habits that slowly shape you into someone dependable, respected, and deeply valued.

The Core Idea

Tomorrow morning, pick just one of these ten rules and practise it consciously for the entire day. Arrive five minutes early. Double-check your work. Finish a long-pending task. One small act of professionalism practised consistently is more powerful than ten philosophies forgotten by evening.

Acknowledgements

A book may be written by one person, but it is shaped by many. This one is no exception.

To my parents: everything begins with you. You gave me life, and you showed me how to live it.

To my wife, Lavleen, my strongest pillar and most honest critic. Thank you for your unwavering support and clarity. You are the quiet strength behind every dream and the reason every achievement feels meaningful.

To my daughters, Kritika and Misha, watching you grow has taught me more than I ever expected. You keep me curious, grounded, and aware that learning never really stops.

To my sons-in-law, Ashit and Karl, thank you for the warmth, respect, and fresh perspectives you bring to our family. And to my grandsons, Kartik and Kshitij, you are gentle reminders that wisdom is best passed on with love, never imposed.

I am deeply grateful to the Spiritual Gurus who have guided and blessed me, often silently and from afar.

To Ajay, my brother-in-law and trusted advisor, your counsel has always been steady and rooted in genuine care.

To Sahil, thank you for your reliability and your quiet, consistent encouragement.

To Shubhra Krishan, my creative partner on this journey, this book found its voice because you helped me find mine.

To the many authors, thinkers, and writers whose words have shaped how I see life, your influence runs through these pages even where your names do not appear.

To my extended family, teachers, mentors, friends, among them Rakesh, Anil, and Nitesh, and even the strangers whose words or silences left a mark on me: this book carries something of each of you.

If these pages offer even one reader a moment of clarity, comfort, or courage, the journey will have been worthwhile.

Rajneesh Jain